Dalesman's
Tea Shop Walks

on the

NORTH YORK MOORS
AND COAST

Mark Reid

25 scenic walks including
traditional tea shops

D1343212

Dalesman

Dalesman Publishing
The Water Mill, Broughton Hall,
Skipton, North Yorkshire BD23 3AG
www.dalesman.co.uk

First Edition 2000
Reprinted 2005

Text © Mark Reid, 2000
Illustrations © Donald Dakeyne
Maps by Jeremy Ashcroft
Cover: by Geoff Cowton

A British Library Cataloguing-in-Publication record
is available for this book

ISBN 1 85568 167 6

Printed in China

PUBLISHER'S NOTE
....

The information given in this book has been provided in good faith and is
intended only as a general guide. Whilst all reasonable efforts have been
made to ensure that details were correct at the time of publication, the
author and Dalesman Publishing cannot accept any responsibility for
inaccuracies. It is the responsibility of individuals undertaking outdoor
activities to approach the activity with caution and, especially if
inexperienced, to do so under appropriate supervision. The activity
described in this book is strenuous and individuals should ensure that they
are suitably fit before embarking upon it. They should carry the appropriate
equipment and maps, be properly clothed and have adequate footwear.
They should also take note of weather conditions and forecasts, and leave
notice of their intended route and estimated time of return.

Dalesman's
Tea Shop Walks

on the

NORTH YORK MOORS AND COAST

Mark Reid

This book is dedicated to my little nephew, Cameron, in the hope that he may follow in my footsteps one day.

Thank you to Stewart and Bernadette Reid, Geoff Temperton, Richard Teasdale, Rachel Gospel, Jane Roberts, Patrick and James Green for being my walking companions over the last year.

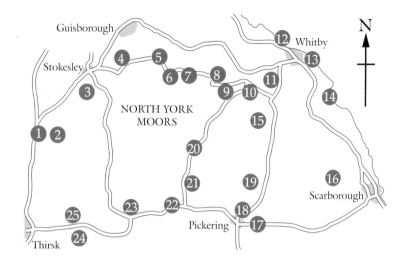

Safety

Never underestimate the strenuous nature of walking, particularly when this is combined with high ground and the elements. Obtain a detailed weather forecast before setting out on your walk, and turn back if the weather turns bad. The temperature, wind speed and general weather conditions on exposed moorland can vary significantly from the conditions at valley level. Your boots are important – make sure that they are waterproof, comfortable and have good ankle support and sturdy soles. Travel light and ensure you have appropriate food and drink, waterproof and windproof clothing with you. Take Ordnance Survey maps (1:25,000) of the area and a compass. Ensure that you keep to Rights of Way and take care when walking along roads or crossing railway lines and rivers.

Always walk in a group unless you are very experienced and inform someone of you intended route and report your safe arrival. Do not attempt to complete a walk that is beyond your skill, experience or level of fitness. Do not explore old mine or quarry workings.

WALKS

INTRODUCTION

With a blaze of publicity it was announced recently that walking is officially the number one leisure activity in this country, but what is its allure? Surely walking is something you do to get from one place to another; a basic human instinct if you will, somewhere akin to breathing and talking. Any experienced walker will tell you that it is not the actual process of putting one foot in front of the other, it is all about the 'walking experience'; but quiz them further to be more precise and they will probably reply, 'Just get out there and try it!'

The North York Moors are special and stand as England's largest remaining expanse of heather moorland. This is walking country par excellence with wonderful paved trods across heather-clad ridges, bracing coastal paths and delectable valley routes. And, best of all, due to the rather modest height of the moors, breathtaking views can be yours for relatively little effort. If you are blessed with a fine day, nothing in this world can beat the feeling of freedom and exhilaration that envelops you as you stand on the top of a rolling heather moor, the wide open spaces, bracing scented air and a sense of history all around. It is this undisturbed history that makes walking so pleasurable as here you will find intact Roman roads, Bronze Age burial mounds, monastic guideposts plus much, much more. People have been living on these moors for over 4,000 years and to make the jigsaw complete you need to talk to the locals and listen to how they interpret the landscape, their dialect and traditions. Suitably tired after a day on the hills, seek out that bastion of British culture, the tea shop, and listen and observe over a steaming cuppa and a slice of home-made cake – you will have deserved it, just make sure you have done the walk first!

*O*smotherley is undoubtedly one of the finest villages in the North of England, surrounded by countryside of unrivalled beauty.

TEA SHOP
The Coffee Pot
Northend
Osmotherley
Tel: 01609 883536
OPEN:
Open daily in summer, Thurs – Sun in winter
MAP:
OS Outdoor Leisure Map 26
DISTANCE:
4½ miles (7.2km)
ALLOW:
2 hours
PARKING:
Ample on-street parking at Osmotherley

It is hard to believe that the busy A19, not to mention the industrial sprawl of Teesside, is only a stone's throw away from the quiet and unspoilt village of Osmotherley. It was a Viking named Osmund who first made his clearing here 1,000 years ago and over the centuries the village grew as a trading centre for the surrounding area, although the market is now only a distant memory. An assortment of attractive stone cottages, complete with their ubiquitous red pantiles, look out across the old market place at the centre of which stands an imposing stone obelisk. Look closely and you will also see a stone table set on squat

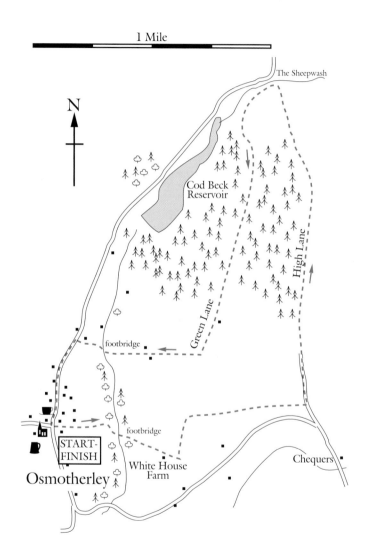

legs, which was once used as a trader's stall; John Wesley, not the tallest fellow by all accounts, used it as an impromptu pulpit on one of his many visits to the village. Nonconformist worship gained a strong foothold in the North York Moors following the Reformation as local people, reluctant to give up their Catholic faith, rejected the Established Church in favour of Nonconformist teachings, a tradition that still continues today. Hidden away along a passageway is Osmotherley's Methodist Chapel, which was built in 1754, making it one of the earliest Methodist chapels in England. Everywhere you go in the North York Moors you will find examples of the power and influence of the Old Faith, and Osmotherley is no exception. A mile or so from the village are the impressive ruins of Mount Grace Priory, a Carthusian priory founded in 1398 that accrued great wealth from vast estates until its dissolution on the orders of Henry VIII.

From the centre of Osmotherley head along the passageway adjacent to the war memorial that leads to Osmotherley Methodist Chapel, after which cross over the lane and follow the walled path opposite that soon brings you out of the village. Follow the clear path across fields, through a kissing gate and down steps to cross a footbridge over Cod Beck.

You may have noticed several long distance footpath signposts, which will come as no surprise when you realise that Osmotherley is the starting point for the gruelling 42-mile Lyke Wake Walk, to be undertaken within 24 hours, and is also en route of the 110-mile Cleveland Way.

From Cod Beck the path heads straight up the hillside to

pass to the left of White House Farm, then continues along the farm track to reach a gate at a T-junction of tracks. Turn left here along the rougher track and follow this steadily upwards. The aches and pains are soon rewarded by superb views across the rooftops of Osmotherley towards the broad acres of the Vale of Mowbray. After the track has levelled out look out for a stile on your right next to a gate (waymarker) that leads on to a track enclosed on one side by a stone wall and on the other by gorse. Follow the track up alongside the wall and continue to head straight on across the now level grassy moorland until you come to a stile on your right that leads onto a clear track which you follow to reach a metalled road. This is true Moors country with the deep ravine of Slape Stones Beck down to the right and in the distance the heather-clad bulks of Black Hambleton and Arden Great Moor fading into the horizon. Turn left along the road and follow it for almost one and a half miles – it becomes increasingly rougher – all the way down to the small ford over Cod Beck known as The Sheepwash.

High Lane is part of Hambleton Street – once an important drovers' road between Scotland and the market towns of York, Malton and beyond. For centuries great herds of livestock, in particular cattle, were taken on hoof to the more prosperous southern markets until the arrival of the railways made the drover redundant. This is one of the oldest roads in the country dating back to pre-Roman times. Such high-level routes avoided the more dangerous valley roads, and proved useful later on as they also avoided the tolls of the turnpike roads. The Sheepwash is a popular Sunday picnic spot with ford, bridge and meandering stream set in idyllic moorland surroundings, although it can get very busy on a warm summer's day.

Do not cross the ford but turn left along the stream for a very short distance then climb up the stony path through the bracken and heather to the top of the bank. With a bird's eye view of The Sheepwash down to your right, follow the path along the edge of the bank, then as you near the plantation bear left away from the stream along a clear path through the heather to reach a ladder stile that leads in to the plantation (sign 'Yorkshire Water Cod Beck Reservoir'). Cross the stile and head straight on through the forest along the path that soon becomes a clear track, grassy at first then stony. Continue straight on ignoring the track down to the right that leads to Cod Beck Reservoir, although if time permits this makes a pleasant diversion, ideal for a picnic. Follow the track straight on, through double gates, then on passing to the right of some farm buildings. The track now becomes a grassy lane, which you follow through metal gates then immediately before the next wooden gate with the stile next to it, take the gate to the right (no signpost). Head straight downhill alongside the fence, passing to the right of the farmhouse to join a farm track, then follow this steeply down to cross over Cod Beck via the footbridge to the right of the road bridge. Follow the track up to reach the road where you turn left back to Osmotherley.

As you enter the village note the stone pinfold on the right, a relic of the days when most land in the area was common and so stray animals were penned up only being released after paying a fine to the Lord of the Manor.

CHEQUERS TEA ROOM

NR OSMOTHERLEY

A walk back in time along one of Britain's oldest roads incorporating an ancient drovers' inn.

TEA SHOP
Chequers Tea
Room
Osmotherley
Tel: 01609 883291
OPEN:
Open daily in
summer, week-
ends Nov – Feb.
MAP:
OS Outdoor
Leisure Map 26
DISTANCE:
3 miles (4.8 km)
ALLOW:
1½ hours
PARKING:
Parking at Square
Corner, grid
reference 479959

You may be a little confused to see the sign outside the Chequers Tea Room, 'Be not in haste, Step in and taste, Ale tomorrow for nothing', as the strongest brew you will find here is a well-stewed cuppa. For centuries the Chequers Inn was a welcome hostelry for the constant stream of drovers along Hambleton Street. This ancient drovers' road stretched from Scotland to the important markets of York, Malton and from there the South of England. During the 18th and 19th centuries it was one of the busiest roads in Britain with mile upon mile of cattle, pigs, geese, sheep and turkeys on their way to market; however, the arrival of the railways heralded the terminal decline of the drovers. This route was in use well before the days of droving and dates back to prehistoric times. You too can follow in the footsteps of Bronze Age people, Romans, Vikings, monks and drovers; it is said that William the Conqueror came this way after his Harrying of the North in 1069.

From the parking area turn left along the road then at the sharp bend head along the clear gravel path, signed 'Cleveland Way, Osmotherley 2 miles' down towards Osmotherley.

This is where the Hambleton Hills meet the Cleveland Hills, both of which combine to form a continuous escarpment running for over 40 miles from Ampleforth to Guisborough, with bleak moorland rising to over 400 metres above sea level from the flat and fertile plains of York, Mowbray and Cleveland. This escarpment provides some of the finest views in England with the Pennines forming a backdrop to a far-reaching vista of farmland; it is said that you can watch a train leave York station and follow it all the way to Darlington from the Hambleton Hills.

This very clear path, with pitched stone steps in places, drops steeply down the heather-clad hillside into the

13

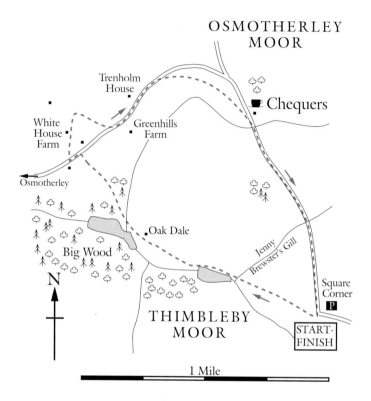

OSMOTHERLEY
MOOR

Trenholm
House

Chequers

White
House
Farm

Greenhills
Farm

Osmotherley

Oak Dale

Big Wood

Jenny
Brewster's Gill

N

Square
Corner

P

THIMBLEBY
MOOR

START-
FINISH

1 Mile

confines of Oak Dale. Follow the path into woodland
and cross the footbridge to reach Oakdale Upper
Reservoir. The path now becomes a wide track running
along the right hand side of the reservoir, then down to
the left of a house, over a bridge and steeply up through
woodland, passing the entrance to Oakdale Lower
Reservoir, to reach the road. Turn left down the road

then after a few yards follow the track up to the right, signed 'Cleveland Way', until you reach the entrance to White House Farm. Continue straight ahead along the less clear track then almost immediately head through the narrow stone wall gap hidden in the hedge on your right (before the metal gate on the right). Keeping the hedge on your left, head straight on across the field to join the road through a gate. Turn left and follow the road up over a cattle grid passing Greenhills Farm. Just after the stone wall has ended on your right take the path that veers away from the road to the right, indicated by a signpost, across the open moor to join the road again at the Chequers.

Once an inn and still a working farm, the Chequers Tea Room is justly famous for its home-made scones that simply melt in your mouth. The Chequers is the oldest inn-sign in Britain as the Romans used to paint a chequers board on the doors of their 'Tabernae' or taverns to indicate the game could be played there. A warm and welcoming atmosphere has greeted travellers here for generations and it is said that a peat fire burned continuously for over 200 years until the 1960s; sadly the last pint of ale was poured in 1945.

Turn right along the road, over Jenny Brewster's Gill, and follow the unfenced moorland road back to the start.

LORD STONES CAFÉ

From the escarpment of the Cleveland Hills a vast panorama across Teesside is spread out before you.

TEA SHOP
Lord Stones Café
Carlton Bank
Nr. Stokesley
Tel: 01642 778227
OPEN:
Daily all year
(excluding
Christmas and
New Year's Day)
MAP:
OS Outdoor
Leisure Map 26
DISTANCE:
4 miles (6.4 km)
ALLOW:
2 hours
PARKING:
Large car park at
café

By far the most unusual café to be found within the North York Moors, this subterranean tea shop certainly blends in with its surroundings; the only give-away is the adjacent car park. Just behind the café lie the remains of the original Three Lords Stone, which once marked the spot where the vast estates of Lords Duncombe of Helmsley, Marwood of Busby Hall and Aylesbury of Snilesworth met centuries ago. It is also the site of some Bronze Age burial mounds, or tumuli, from where many flint arrowheads dating back over 5,000 years were discovered, which can now be seen on display in the café.

From the café car park head out away from the road towards the escarpment, turning right after the small copse dedicated to 'Alec and Annie Falconer 1970' and along the wide grassy path. The clear path, pitched with stone steps, climbs steeply up alongside the stone wall and fence to the top of Cringle Moor.

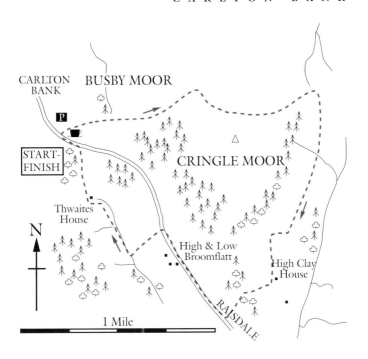

What a view! And such a thoughtful place to build a seat and windbreak, complete with brass viewfinder to the 'Memory of Alec Falconer 1884 – 1968, Rambler'. Beneath your feet the escarpment of the Cleveland Hills plunges over 300 metres to the flat Vale of Cleveland, with Roseberry Topping and Teesside clearly visible as well as Swaledale, Ingleborough and even Durham Cathedral on a very clear day.

Follow the clear path along the top of the escarpment with exhilarating views down to your left and heather moorland sweeping away to your right surmounted by a large burial mound known as Drake Howe; 'howe' is the Old Norse word for burial mound. After a while the path begins its descent down into Raisdale, gently at first and then very steeply to the bottom of the valley where it meets a stone wall. Turn right along this wall through an area of spoil heaps to reach a gate (waymarkers).

The scars caused by centuries of mining and quarrying for jet, ironstone and alum can still be seen throughout the North York Moors. Alum was extensively mined in this area, particularly during the 17th to 19th centuries, and was used in the textile and tanning industries.

Keep alongside the stone wall, passing a gate in the wall on your left, soon after which the path becomes boggy and unclear through bracken. Continue alongside the wall until a waymarker points you slightly to the right away from the wall. You must now pick your way through the bracken and young trees heading up a slight bank to join the wall again, which is now bending up to the right as well (you should now be opposite the farm on the other side of the valley). Follow the much clearer path alongside the wall, marked by waymarkers, until you reach a tumbledown wall and old stone gatepost across your path. Head right here up alongside the wall to the top of the hill, then left along a track to reach a gate. Immediately before the gate turn left through a large wall gap and follow the overgrown track alongside the stone wall down to reach High Clay Farm. Keep to the right of the farm buildings to join the farm track by a small pond and follow the track all the way to reach the road. Turn right along the road for half a mile, passing Low and High Broomflatt Farms, reposing in their idyllic location at the head of the little-known Raisdale, tributary of Bilsdale. 200 yards or so after the turning for High Broomflatt Farm turn left through a gate to 'Staindale Farm' and follow the track down through a gate; then as the track bears away down to the left take the path to the right, marked by a signpost and head towards the corner of the stone wall opposite. Walk alongside this wall, over a railway sleeper footbridge after which bear left down a path to cross the beck over another footbridge and up to a stile. Cross the stile then bear slightly to the left up the hill away from the beck, across the field, to reach a gate in the far left-hand corner of the field. Head up to join a farm track where you turn right and follow this track passing Thwaites House to reach the road. Lord Stones Café is a short walk to your left along the road.

GLEBE COTTAGE

K I L D A L E

The brisk climb to the breezy heights of Easby Moor is more than compensated by the unsurpassed views across 'Captain Cook Country'.

TEA SHOP
Glebe Cottage
Station Road
Kildale
Tel: 01642 724470
OPEN:
Every day, all year.
MAP:
OS Outdoor
Leisure Map 26
DISTANCE:
4½ miles (7.2 km)
ALLOW:
2 hours
PARKING:
Limited on-street parking

The tiny village of Kildale lies hidden amongst the Cleveland Hills, a cluster of houses along a minor road that is certainly 'off the beaten track'; however, for such a small place it has a fascinating history. For over 900 years the Kildale Estate has been in the hands of only three families, the most influential of which was the Percy family. The earthworks of their original 12th century motte and bailey castle can still be seen near to St Cuthbert's Church. The original boundaries have not altered over the intervening centuries and much of the village and surrounding moorland is still owned by the Lord of the Manor, who now resides at the imposing Kildale Hall. When St Cuthbert's Church was rebuilt in 1868 several Viking graves were discovered which held swords, daggers and even battleaxes, indicating that this has been a place of worship since Saxon times, although these Vikings were most probably pagans buried within this sacred site. Inside the porch are some beautiful ancient tombstones carved with the Percy emblem. Before starting this walk spare a moment to look at the prime contender for the smallest train station in the country as well as the well-stocked and friendly village shop, a rarity nowadays.

From the road junction in the centre of Kildale turn down the side road towards the station then take the first turning on your right passing Glebe Cottage, marked 'Cleveland Way'. Follow this lane down under the railway bridge, over a cattle grid and across meadowland then up to the right towards Bankside Farm. As the road bends sharply to the right at Bankside Cottage turn to the left through the higher of the two gates that leads into Mill Bank Wood.

This whole area once was a centre for the mining of jet, whinstone and iron ore and many of the hillsides, including Easby Moor, are still scarred by the old workings.

Head straight on along the clear forest track then after three quarters of a mile veer away from the clear track along a less distinct bridleway, marked by a signpost. The path soon leaves the confines of the forest and heads straight on across the flanks of Easby Moor alongside a stone wall all the way to Ayton Banks Wood. To your left are exhilarating views across the Vale of Cleveland towards the escarpment of the Cleveland Hills. A clear path leads straight through this next plantation to a gate at the other end of the wood, after which carry straight on with rough heathland and open woodland on your right and superb views to your left until you reach an open grassy area with Roseberry Topping in front of you. Bear up to the right across the grassy hillside to reach a gate that leads back into dense forest. After the gate head up through the woods along a clear but extremely steep path, with steps in parts to ease the climb. The path eventually leaves the forest at the top of Easby Moor and leads straight on to Captain Cook's Monument.

Visible for miles around, this 50-foot monument stands as a sentinel above the Vale of Cleveland. Built as a memorial to Captain James Cook, a tablet explains the circumstances behind its building in 1827, albeit in rather amusing antiquated Victorian language. Captain Cook was born in 1728 at Marton, now a suburb of Middlesbrough, and later went to school at Great Ayton. In 1746 he started his maritime apprenticeship at Whitby, a career path that would later make him this country's most famous explorer and seafarer.

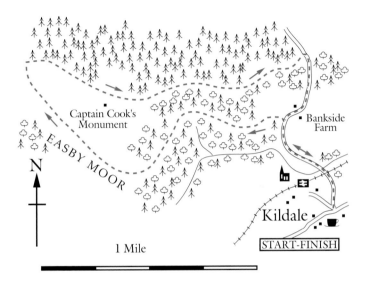

A clear path leads straight on from the Monument in the direction that you had been walking, then drops steeply down a pitched stone path alongside a plantation on your left and enters the forest. A clear track now heads through the forest – ignore any paths that branch off to the left – to eventually join a very clear forest track which brings you out on a road. Turn right and follow this road down passing Bankside Farm after which retrace your steps back into Kildale.

THE OLD POST OFFICE TEA ROOMS

C O M M O N D A L E

The Esk Valley Railway provides a comforting companion during this walk across the flanks of Commondale Moor.

TEA SHOP
The Old Post
Office Tea Rooms
Commondale
Nr Castleton
Tel: 01287 660060
OPEN:
Every day from
April until Oct
MAP:
OS Outdoor
Leisure 26
DISTANCE:
3¹/₂ miles (5.6 km)
ALLOW:
1¹/₂ hours
PARKING: Small
car park near the
church for tea
shop customers

Narrow moorland roads lead steeply down into the confines of Raven Gill and the surprising sight of brick built houses, a church and an old school. The bricks seem slightly out of place in this moorland setting and, I am sorry to say, give a rather unattractive appearance to Commondale. With the arrival of the railway in the 1860s came industrial activity in the form of a brick works, which continued in production until the late 1940s. Commondale is encircled by mile upon mile of dramatic moorland, which will reveal, for the trained eye, dozens of Iron and Bronze Age remains including earthworks, dykes, enclosures, burial mounds and even a stone circle dating back to prehistoric times.

From the crossroads in the centre of the village follow the road down towards the station then after only a very short distance turn left along a grassy bridleway which passes to the right of the tea rooms heading up alongside the wall. Follow this path up the hillside, paved in places, through three gates

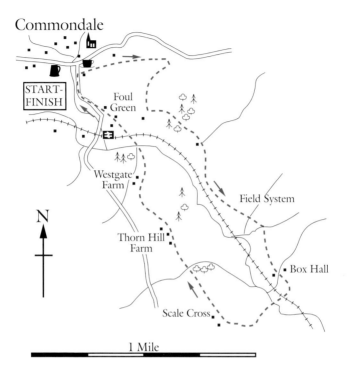

and then bear right up across the moorland along a clear paved path, with the beautiful valley of Commondale Beck, not Esk Dale as some people believe, down to your right.

Commondale developed at the crossroads of several ancient routes across the moors, indeed the name may originate from 'Colman's Valley' because, according to local folklore, Colman, the Bishop of Lindisfarne, once stopped here en route to Whitby Abbey. Numerous tracks radiate from this village, some of which date back to prehistoric times including the famous Quakers' trod, a superb paved path across the moors that once connected Guisborough Priory with Whitby Abbey and Rosedale Priory.

Just before the path joins the stone wall head through the gate in the wall on the right and drop down the hillside across rough rocky ground to reach a stone wall across your path. Turn left through a gate and follow the wall down through another gate and on to a clear farm track where you turn left to reach a small group of cottages. Keep to the track above the houses along the side of the valley and follow this now much rougher track for three-quarters of a mile until you come to Box Hall. Continue along the track for approximately 100 yards after Box Hall then turn off the track to the right through a gate and head down the field and over a path across the railway line – ensure that you stop, look and listen!

After the railway crossing continue straight on across the field and down over Commondale Beck by either a footbridge or ford then follow the grassy track straight up the hillside to reach a farm track across your path. Follow this track to the right through a gate and up to reach Scale Cross Farm, where you turn right through a gate immediately before the farm buildings. Head along the path keeping close to the stone wall on your left through another gate, then head along the grassy track across fields through two more gates to join a clearer track. Follow this clearer track to the left across a small stream then up to reach Thorn Hill Farm. Continue along the track passing to the right of the farm buildings, through a gate at the end of the farmyard then straight on along the less distinct track across grassland towards Westgate Farm. Just before you reach the farm buildings cross the ladder stile over the wall to your right then veer left down the hillside passing through a gate that leads behind the farm buildings, after which turn right through another gate and head straight downhill to a ladder stile. After the stile the path drops steeply down to cross a footbridge over Commondale Beck and then crosses the railway line once again via stiles – remember to take care. Just after the railway line you come to a tumbledown wall, immediately after which turn left alongside the wall and fence and then up to cross over a ladder stile that leads on to the road above the station.

The Esk Valley Railway was saved from Beeching's infamous axe due to the concerted efforts of people from Whitby and Esk Dale who feared the loss of an essential lifeline to the outside world. There are twelve small stations along this picturesque railway line between Middlesbrough and Whitby, each one vying for the title of 'Smallest Station'; Commondale Station, with its tiny waiting room, has a strong claim for the title.

Follow the road back up into Commondale, passing two large ponds on your left.

CASTLETON TEA ROOMS

CASTLETON

A short but fascinating walk in the heart of upper Esk Dale from the site of a Norman fortress.

TEA SHOP
The Castleton Tea Rooms
Church Street
Castleton
Tel: 01287 660135
OPEN:
Every day from Easter until end Oct, weekends in winter
MAP:
OS Outdoor Leisure Map 26
DISTANCE:
3 miles (4.8 km)
ALLOW:
1¹/₂ hours
PARKING:
On-street parking in the centre of Castleton

Castleton lies near the confluence of Commondale Beck and the River Esk at the point where four dales converge to form Esk Dale; the infant River Esk flows through Westerdale until it reaches Castleton. The Normans chose this strategically important site for a wooden castle to help subjugate the unruly North following the Conquest. All that remains of this stronghold is a tree-clad earthen mound just off Station Road. Although its market is no more than a memory, Castleton is still the principal village of the upper dale with a variety of shops and interesting buildings of varying architectural styles, which straddle the road as it climbs up onto the windswept heights of Castleton Rigg.

From the centre of Castleton, walk up the main High Street passing the Moorlands Inn on your left and out of the village. To your right are extensive views across Esk Dale and down towards Castleton's station

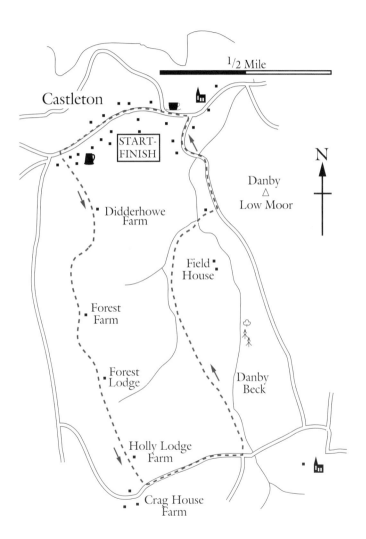

1/2 Mile

Castleton

START-FINISH

Danby
△
Low Moor

N

Didderhowe
Farm

Field
House

Forest
Farm

Forest
Lodge

Danby
Beck

Holly Lodge
Farm

Crag House
Farm

and cricket ground. Just before the road bends to the left as you leave the village turn left along a track towards Didderhowe Farm and follow the track down to reach the farm. Follow the footpath to the left of the farm buildings and cross over a stile by a gate, after which turn right following the fence and wall round to the left and then through two successive gates.

After the gates head up the hillside to your right to reach a stile in the wall at the top of the field. Cross the stile and turn left along the wall and up to join a farm track above Forest Farm. Turn left down the track into the farmyard then before you reach the farmhouse head through the gate on your right opposite the haybarns and walk up across the field to a ladder stile above the farmhouse which leads on to a rough track. Turn left

along the track and follow it down to reach Forest Lodge Farm, head through the gate into the farmyard then take the gate on the right before the farmhouse, after which head left passing above the farmhouse to reach an old wall stile in the corner of the field. A clear path now heads straight on through a series of gates to reach Holly Lodge Farm.

Esk Dale is fed by many smaller valleys that predominantly run south to north. Danby Dale is one of the largest tributary valleys and strikes deep into the heart of the Moors, separated from its neighbouring valleys by Castleton Rigg and Danby Rigg. Ancient tracks criss-cross these ridges, or riggs, which are scattered with Bronze and Iron Age remains. Our path passes a string of farmhouses that run along the western flanks of the dale, each with their own distinct architectural style, some of which date back several centuries.

Continue straight on passing the farm on your left and through a gate after the farmhouse then, keeping the wall on your right, head straight on, over a stile and through a gate to the left of Crag House Farm that leads onto the road. Turn left and follow the road down to the bottom of the hill, with the church in the distance, then head through a gate on the left, marked 'Castleton', opposite the road turning on the right before you reach the bridge over Danby Beck.

St Hilda's Church stands in splendid isolation half way up Danby Dale and some considerable distance from the village of Danby and was, according to folklore, built using stones from Castleton's castle. Solitary churches are good indicators of deserted villages and it is possible that this was the site of the original village. Canon Atkinson, the famous vicar of

Danby who wrote 'Forty years in a Moorland Parish', lies buried in the churchyard.

Keeping close to the river on your right at first, head across the field and through a gate, after which follow the grassy track straight on through a series of gates leaving the river behind. After a while the track runs alongside a small stream on your left and becomes less distinct, although the gates provide adequate guidance across the fields. The track gradually bends round to the right, still heading alongside the stream, then crosses a bridge over Danby Beck after which a clearly marked path skirts to the right around Brookfield Farm to join the road. Turn left and follow the road back into Castleton.

THE MOORS TEA ROOM

THE MOORS CENTRE, DANBY

This walk explores the history of Esk Dale, from the Bronze Age remains on Danby Rigg to the crumbling ruins of Danby Castle.

TEA ROOM
The Moors Tea Room, The Moors Centre Danby Lodge Danby
Tel: 01287 660654
OPEN:
Every day Mar – Dec; weekends only Jan – Feb
MAP:
OS Outdoor Leisure 27
DISTANCE:
7 miles (11.3 km)
ALLOW: 3 hours
PARKING: Large pay and display car park at the Moors Centre

Danby, also called Danby-in-Cleveland or Danby End, lies at the mouth of its own small dale. The name Danby literally means the village of the Danes, although they were not the first people to settle in this area as the surrounding moors are littered with physical reminders of Bronze and Iron Age peoples. The Moors Centre is housed in Danby Lodge, a 17th century shooting lodge owned by the Dawnay family who bought the Manor of Danby in 1656. As well as a shop, information point and tea room there is also an interesting display area which provides a fascinating insight into the evolution of the landscape of the North York Moors, as well as the many pressures now facing this wonderful National Park.

From the car park turn right along the road passing the entrance to the Moors Centre then follow the footpath to the right immediately after the road junction behind the

Moors Centre buildings. Follow the clear path up through the wood to reach a gate, after which continue along the grassy track ahead, keeping alongside the stone wall on your left. Before you reach the end of the wall, head left through a gate in the wall and follow the clear path up to the top of the hill where the path joins a track down into the village of Danby. Turn right along the road into the village, then left at the road junction and follow the road down over the railway and River Esk. At the bridge over the Esk, look to the right and you will see the 17th century Esk Mill.

The swift waters of the Esk once provided power for several mills; however, this is the last remaining working watermill where visitors can still see grain being milled.

Continue along the road then take the turning on the left opposite the fire station into Ainthorpe, a quiet village situated on the south slopes of Esk Dale with an assortment of old cottages and farms, village green complete with quoits pitch and a pub that dates back to 1555. Follow the road up through the village, passing the pub on your left, and out onto the moors. Just after the tennis court where the road bends to the left, follow the bridleway to the right across the heather moorland, marked by a signpost, and head up the clear narrow track to reach a gate. The clear path now heads straight on climbing steadily up across Danby Rigg for three-quarters of a mile until you reach the ridge above Little Fryup Dale.

Danby Rigg has one of the greatest concentrations of Bronze and Iron Age remains in the country with over 800 cairns, earthworks, double and single dykes, enclosures, settlement and field systems, and a stone circle of which only one massive standing stone remains, all of which dates back 3,000 years.

You come across the view from Danby Rigg across Little Fryup Dale rather unexpectedly; however, the surprise is one of delight as this is undoubtedly one of the finest views in the North York Moors. The exquisitely named Little Fryup Dale

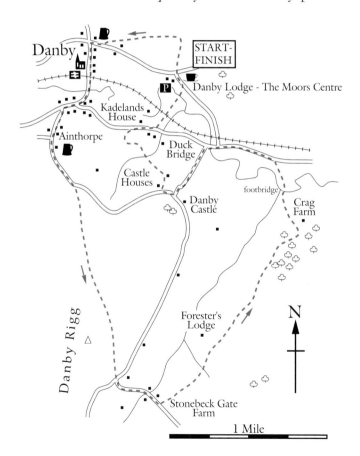

has nothing to do with the breakfast fare at local B&Bs, but is derived from the old English personal name 'Friga' and 'up' meaning valley.

From the ridge follow the path bearing to the right steeply down the hillside to join the road at the bottom of the valley near to the road junction. At the road head straight on (ignore the road up to the right and down to the left) and follow the road between two farms, then past some farm buildings. Turn left along the bridleway passing in front of Stonebeck Gate Farm and follow the clear stony track for half a mile.

Where the track turns down to the left towards Forester's Lodge, head straight on through the gate, marked by a signpost, and follow the grassy track through a series of gates across several fields for one mile to reach Crag Farm. As you approach the farm, turn left at a signpost down through a gate in the fence and on to a track. Head straight on through the gate opposite and follow the overgrown track passing in front of the farmhouse to join a metalled farm track which you follow up to the main road. Turn left along the road – take care as this can be busy in summer – then as the road bends to the right take the turning to the left down to reach Duck Bridge.

This graceful stone packhorse bridge was originally built in 1396, although extensively repaired in the 18th century by George Duck, hence the name. If you look carefully you will notice the coat of arms of the Neville family who owned the Manor of Danby in the 15th century. Amazingly it was still used by cars until 1993 when a ford was built making a somewhat easier crossing over the Esk.

After the bridge, turn left and follow the road up to Danby Castle.

Dating from the early 14th century, Danby Castle was built by Lord Latimer as a sign of his wealth and power, not for defence, as he owned vast estates throughout Esk Dale and wanted to parade his wealth to the common folk of the dale. It is said that Katherine Parr, sixth wife of Henry VIII, once lived at the castle. Today it is a working farm with the farmhouse incorporated into one of the four original corner towers. This is where the ancient Danby Court Leet still meets, a throwback to feudal times.

In 1655 the manor of Danby was sold off with many of the tenant farmers buying their farms, who subsequently set up a locally elected body to control the use of the common land. Most Court Leets declined after the Enclosure Acts; however, Danby Court Leet has continued to flourish and still has powers to fine people for encroachment upon the common.

The ruins, which lie on private land, are impressive with arches, crumbling towers and walls as well as commanding views of Esk Dale.

Take the road turning to the right just before the Castle, then after a short distance follow the footpath to the right through a gate, marked by a signpost, and follow the path down towards Castle Houses Farm. When you reach the main farm buildings, turn left and follow the track to reach a ladder stile next to a gate, after which bear to the right down to a gate in the far right corner of the field. After the gate head straight up the slight incline and across the field to join a path running along a hedge. Turn left alongside the hedge, through a kissing gate, then turn right to reach the road where you head right passing Kadelands Farm. Then just after the house on the right, take the path to the left signposted 'Danby Lodge', and follow the clear path over the railway line (remember to take care) and footbridge back to the Moors Centre.

SHEPHERD'S HALL
TEA ROOMS

L E A L H O L M

A short but exhilarating walk from one of the prettiest villages in Yorkshire up onto expansive heather moorland with breathtaking views.

TEA ROOM
Shepherd's Hall
Tea Rooms
Lealholm
Tel: 01947 87361
OPEN:
Every day Mar –
Dec, closed Jan &
Feb.
MAP:
OS Outdoor
Leisure Map 27
DISTANCE:
4 miles (6.4 km)
ALLOW:
2 hours
PARKING:
Large car park in
village centre

Lealholm, pronounced locally 'Lealum', is perhaps the prettiest village in the North York Moors, although contenders are many. Try to imagine an idyllic English country village and you would not be far from reality at Lealholm. A time-mellowed stone bridge spans the River Esk, next to which stands an old-fashioned village pub. A little further along the river, stepping stones take the more adventurous person across the Esk, especially after heavy rain. Village life is thriving here with an amazing village shop that sells just about everything, Post Office, school, churches of various denominations including Catholic, Anglican and Methodist, garage, station, tea room and sprawling village green kept trim by jaywalking sheep who will quite happily share your sandwiches! Quoits is still popular in the North York Moors, in particular Esk Dale, and Lealholm is no exception; stand and watch awhile, for this game requires a great deal of skill and strength. The

Shepherd's Hall Tea Rooms is housed in the old Loyal Order of Ancient Shepherds' Friendly Society, which operated as a type of insurance company for local people before the days of Social Security; it has been a tea shop now for over 20 years.

From the car park at the centre of Lealholm head out along the Danby-Castleton road opposite, then turn right before the garage and Post Office and follow the track up, through a white kissing gate and across the railway line (take care) to reach the station.

The Esk Valley Railway Line, completed in 1865, escaped Beeching's infamous axe mainly due to the fervent opposition from the people of Whitby who feared the loss of all of their train services. At one time four routes radiated out from Whitby – you could catch a train to Scarborough, Pickering, Middlesbrough or Loftus. The Esk Valley Line remains as one of the most scenic railway lines in the country.

Turn left along the road passing the old station on your left, after which head up the track to the right and over a stile by a gate – do not go into the old goods yard. Follow the grassy track up then round to the right as you approach a wall across your path with two gates in it. Keep to the less clear path alongside this wall to reach a signpost at a gate. Do not go over the stile but turn sharp right and drop down to join the clear stony track again, over a small stream then steeply up the hill. Half way up the hill turn left along a grassy track through the heather and bracken, follow this track bearing slightly to the left at the next gate to reach a clear farm track just above Greystones Farm. Turn right and head up the track to reach the road, then turn right along the road. Where the road bends to the right, head straight on across the heather moorland along a paved footpath.

These ancient paved trods are what make walking in the North York Moors so pleasurable – they are simply wonderful to walk on. Many of these paved causeways date from when pannier ponies were the main way goods were transported around the country, and were first laid across the moors in medieval times, although some may date back further. They continued to be used up until the end of the 19th century; note the old guidepost inscribed 'JH 1869'. The views from here are incredible with the splendours of Esk Dale and Great Fryup Dale beneath your feet.

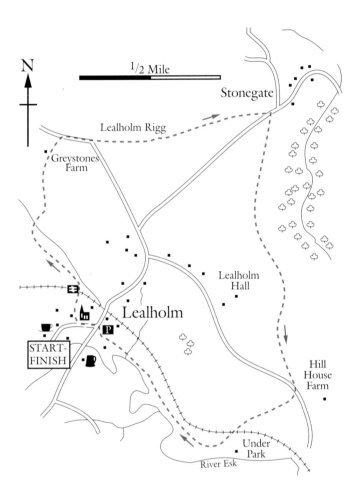

Just before the path reaches the road, the paving stones come to an end – follow the left branch of the paths straight on to join a moorland track adjacent to the road at a signpost. Turn right onto the road, then left towards the group of houses at Stonegate. Just before the houses follow the footpath to the right heading slightly back on yourself and cross over a stile by a gate in the fence. Follow the grassy track alongside the wall, over another stile by a gate then at the next gate follow the track up to the right. After only a short distance head left over a stile by a gate, then walk straight on through a double gate in the tumbledown wall and down to the next gate.

Continue straight on down the hillside alongside the wall on your left, then where the wall ends and the hedge begins swap to walk on the left hand side of the hedge by means of a gap in the wall and follow the hedge down the hillside to reach a small footbridge that heads to the right through the hedge. Cross over the farm track and head across the field bearing slightly to the right to reach a signpost at the corner of a hedge situated at the top of a steep ravine. Follow the hedge down with the ravine on your left to reach the road. Turn left down the road and up a small incline at the top of which take the path to the right through a gate, marked 'bridleway'.

Head straight on along the grassy track with the railway line down to your left, down through a gate, after which the track becomes very clear passing a small duck pond and swings round to the left under the railway line to reach Underpark Farm. At the farmhouse turn right and follow the farm track all the way back to Lealholm.

BEGGAR'S BRIDGE TEA ROOM

G L A I S D A L E

The 'village missed by the Reformation', a 17th century pack-horse bridge with romantic connections and pannier routes through ancient woodland are just some of the highlights on this delightful walk.

TEA SHOP
Beggar's Bridge Tea Room, Glaisdale
Esk Dale
Tel: 01947 897533
OPEN:
Every day Easter until the end of Oct.
MAP:
OS Outdoor Leisure Map 27
DISTANCE:
4 miles (6.4 km)
ALLOW: 2 hours
PARKING
Free car park near Egton Bridge Station.
NB This walk starts at Egton Bridge

At the heart of beautiful Esk Dale lies Egton Bridge, the jewel in the crown of this wonderful valley. The original stone bridge that gave the village its name was washed away by floods in the 1930s, and a temporary iron bridge was constructed that lasted until the new award-winning stone bridge was built in 1993. The North York Moors has many superb monastic ruins whose spiritual and economic influence came to an abrupt end five centuries ago with the Dissolution of the Monasteries. However, people in the North York Moors were reluctant to give up the 'Old Faith' and Catholicism continued, albeit behind closed doors in fear of persecution. Egton Bridge is often referred to as the 'village missed by the Reformation' and remains as one of the most famous Catholic parishes in England. The continuation of the Catholic faith can be

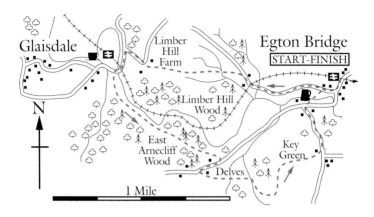

attributed to Father Nicholas Postgate who ministered in this area for over 50 years before he was hanged at York in 1679 aged 82 – his crime was to baptise a child into the Catholic faith. The imposing Catholic Church dedicated to St Hedda was built in 1866 and has a wonderfully ornate ceiling and altar as well as three-dimensional wall pictures inside and out depicting the Stations of the Cross and the life of Jesus. In the shadow of the church stands the much smaller original church that was built in 1795 and now serves as the village school and home of the famous Egton Bridge Annual Gooseberry Show.

From the parking area near to the station turn right and walk down the road passing St Hedda's Church then take the first turning on your right to 'Glaisdale 2'. Follow the well-worn flagged footpath alongside the road and head out of the village passing some fine Victorian houses along the way. The lane soon leaves the houses behind and joins the banks of the River Esk, which is one of the few remaining salmon rivers left in this country, then turns sharply to the right under a railway bridge and climbs uphill passing Broom House.

Halfway up this hill take the path to the left and head across the field keeping close to the fence and wood on your left, with views of Esk Dale beginning to open up behind. Drop down to the left over a small stream then up to the right to a stile that leads into a small wood. Head uphill through the wood and over the stile at the other end, after which walk straight on across the field keeping to the fence on your left to join a track that leads down towards Limber Hill Farm. Forsake the gate that leads into the farmyard for the wide grassy track to the

left; follow this round to the right to reach the road. Turn left down Limber Hill – the North York Moors are noted for their steep and twisting roads and this one-in-three hill is no exception – and cross the River Esk by way of Beggar's Bridge, which has romantic associations.

Thomas Ferris, a local man of few means, regularly made the short journey across the Esk to see his sweetheart; however, her father did not approve of the courtship so Thomas decided to go to sea to make his fortune. Sadly they were prevented from saying goodbye because the swollen River Esk had submerged the stepping stones. He fought against the Armada and eventually became Mayor of Hull, later returning to Glaisdale a rich man. He built this graceful bridge in 1619 so that no other lovers would be separated by the river. Today the bridge is almost hidden by the obtrusive road and rail bridges; however, nothing can detract from the skill of its builders. Beggar's Bridge Tea Room is a short distance along the road to the right, located in the old station buildings.

Walk under the railway bridge and cross the stream directly ahead either by ford or footbridge. Walk up the steps heading up to the left through the woods and follow the old packhorse route, paved in places, through East Arncliff Woods to eventually reach the road. At the road turn right and follow it very steeply uphill, passing The Delves, winding up to the top of the hill, where you take the path to the left through a gate. Head straight on for a short distance then turn left at the waymarker down the hillside, over a stile then down through woodland to reach a farm track. Head straight across the track through the gate opposite and drop downhill keeping the small stream on your left to reach a footbridge. Cross the bridge and bear slightly to the right up the hillside and through a gate in the hedge, after which turn left keeping close to the hedge, over a wooded stream and up the hillside to reach a lane. Turn right and follow the lane up to Hall Grange Farm.

Immediately after the farm buildings turn left through a gate and follow the bridleway straight up the hillside to reach a barn at the top of the hill. Turn left at the barn along a rough track that leads to a gate, after which the track becomes much clearer and bends round to the right to eventually reach farm buildings at Key Green and the road. Turn left and follow the road steeply down back into Egton Bridge.

At the road junction as you enter the village follow the path directly ahead that takes you down over stepping stones across the Esk, a wonderful way to end this walk. After crossing the river follow the path to the right passing the old mill buildings and back on to the road where you turn right and retrace your steps back to the parking area.

HAZLEWOOD TEA ROOMS

GROSMONT

A tour of one of the world's first passenger railway lines engineered by Stephenson and Hudson, pioneers of train travel.

TEA SHOP
Hazlewood Tea
Rooms
Front Street
Grosmont
Tel: 01947 895292
OPEN:
Every day from
Easter until end Oct.
MAP:
OS Outdoor Leisure
Map 27
DISTANCE:
4½ miles (7.2 km)
ALLOW:
2½ hours
PARKING:
Large pay and
display car park at
Grosmont.

If you enjoy steam trains, then Grosmont is the place for you! The famous Grosmont to Pickering line, home of the North Yorkshire Moors Railway, runs through the heart of this village after branching off from the main Esk Dale line between Whitby and Middlesbrough. This preserved railway provides a fascinating insight into the 'Age of Steam' with bridges, level crossing, signal box, old-fashioned station, loco sheds and tunnels, including the world's oldest passenger railway tunnel. The Whitby to Pickering line was completed in 1836 and some 30 years later the line from

Grosmont to Middlesbrough via Esk Dale opened heralding the development of the village. Grosmont was also a major centre for the mining of iron ore as particularly rich deposits were discovered when the Pickering line was being built. At their height these mines produced over 100,000 tons of iron ore that helped feed the blast furnaces of Teesside; however, the mines closed in 1871. Originally the village was rather unimaginatively called 'Tunnel' later being renamed Grosmont after the 13th century priory that once stood nearby, the memory of which continues through the names of local farms and woods.

From the centre of Grosmont walk along the main road towards Whitby, over the level crossing (remember to take care) immediately after which take the footpath to the right towards the 'Loco Shed and Goathland'. The path crosses a footbridge over the Murk Esk then splits, our route veers up to the left signed 'Rail trail' to a kissing gate, after which turn left heading down passing the church on your left. A path turns off to the right just before the graveyard on the right which you follow down over a footbridge and onto a road.

This whole area is an absolute delight hidden away in the confines of the Murk Esk Valley. Thickly wooded slopes, overhanging crags and a playful river combine to create a lovely scene through which a road runs over several very precarious fords; a wonderful place to explore.

Turn right and follow the lane up, through a gate across the road then, after a short distance, veer away from the road to the right along the footpath, paved in places, to reach a small gate that leads into woodland. This old packhorse route heads through the woods along the side of the hill – ignore any paths down or up through the woods – for half a mile until you reach a small footbridge at the end of the woods. After the footbridge follow the path straight on alongside the fence with the valley down to your right

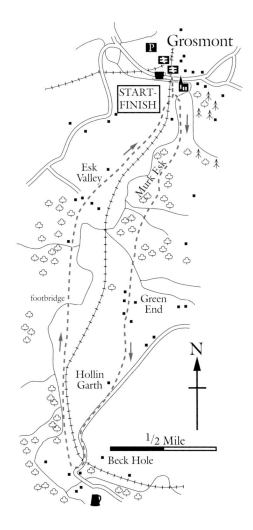

across two fields at the end of which a stile leads over the fence to the right. The path bends to the left, crosses another stile then heads straight on along the top of the field with wonderful views to the right then back into woodland again.

Follow the clear path round to the right over a bridge then up to join a farm track. Turn left through the gate and follow the track towards Green End Farm, then as you approach the farm buildings head straight on along the lane ahead enclosed by tumbledown walls, through two gates and onto a clear farm track. Turn left up along the track then at the last farm building on the right take the track to the right, marked by a signpost, which leads through the farmyard through two gates and onto a rough track that heads straight on from the farmyard.

As the clearer track bends away to the right continue straight on along the grassy track and follow this over a series of stiles and gates keeping close to the wall on your right to reach the road to the left of Hollin Garth Farm. Follow the road to the right, over the railway bridge then very steeply down into Beck Hole.

The only way in, or out, of Beck Hole is via a VERY steep road as the village lies along the floor of a deep valley near to the confluence of Ellerbeck and West Beck which join forces to form the Murk Esk. Old stone cottages look out across a village green where quoits is still played, and beside the bridge over Ellerbeck stands one of the finest country inns in England. The Birch Hall Inn has not altered since the days when it helped slake the thirst of the miners who dug for iron ore in the surrounding hills and retains three tiny rooms one of which is a shop. It also has a unique pub sign painted by Algernon Newton, a member of the

Royal Academy, as a gift for the landlady in return for the many happy evenings he had spent there.

As the road bends round to the left at the bottom of the hill by the village green follow the footpath to the right through a gate to 'Egton Bridge' and follow this clear path as it gradually drops down through woodland to reach a stile by a gate. Follow the path straight on with the river on your left to reach a new footbridge over the river – do not cross this bridge but continue down alongside the river following the old trackbed all the way to the terrace of old miners' cottages at Esk Valley.

This was the original route of George Stephenson's Whitby to Pickering railway line which opened in 1836; however, the section between Grosmont and Goathland was notoriously steep and difficult with the carriages and wagons having to be hauled up the Beck Hole Incline with its one-in-ten gradient. George Hudson converted the line from horse to steam power and in 1865 blasted the 'deviation route' so avoiding this steep incline. The old trackbed is now a popular walk with a great deal to see along the way including the old bridge supports all of which is set in beautiful surroundings.

Continue along the old trackbed now with the 'newer' railway line on your right heading towards Grosmont. You soon pass an area of sidings with a fascinating selection of old engines and rolling stock. A well-marked path skirts to your left above and around the Loco Shed area to reach the junction of paths near to the church where we began our walk. From here retrace your steps back into the village.

RIVER GARDENS CAFÉ

An easy walk that offers unsurpassed views of lower Esk Dale and the hidden valley of Little Beck with a final descent along a superb paved trod.

TEA SHOP
River Gardens Café
The Carrs
Sleights
Tel: 01947 810329
OPEN:
Every day mid March – mid Oct.
MAP:
OS Outdoor Leisure Map 27
DISTANCE:
3 miles (4.8 km)
ALLOW:
1½ hours
PARKING:
Free car park beside the road bridge over the Esk

To many people Sleights is somewhere on the way to Whitby, memorable only for Blue Bank, the long and precariously steep road that drops down from Sleights Moor to cross over the River Esk. There has been a bridge here across the Esk since the 12th century, originally built by the monks of Whitby Abbey. There is not much to catch the eye as you drive into this sprawling village, an eclectic mix of architectural styles; however, the surrounding countryside more than compensates. Lying just to the west of Sleights along the banks of the Esk are the remains of Eskdale Chapel, an ancient place of worship that was once the home of a hermit. In 1159 three men out hunting a boar attacked the hermit as he sheltered the animal, and before he died he imposed a penance on the men. For over 800 years the tradition of the Planting of the Penny Hedge, otherwise known as the Horngarth Ceremony, has taken place once a year. This Ceremony involves the planting of a small woven wooden fence in the mud of Whitby Harbour which must withstand three tides otherwise the lands of the perpetrators, or their successors, would be forfeited to the abbot of Whitby.

From the parking area beside the bridge over the River Esk, turn right along the main road over the road bridge, immediately after which turn left through some gates along a lane, with a signpost pointing to 'Grosmont'. Follow the lane up passing Groves Hall, with the Esk down to your left – note the weir and salmon leap; this is one of England's last remaining salmon rivers. The lane leaves the company of the river to run alongside a small stream then crosses a bridge over this stream to reach Woodlands, a fine late 18th century house built from the proceeds of the alum industry. Continue to follow the lane as it bears up to the right after Woodlands then take the footpath to the left, marked by a signpost. A paved path leads down across the hillside then round to the right to reach Thistle Grove Farm, with wonderful views of Esk Dale before you.

Pass in front of the farmhouse, over a stile and onto the road then turn left and follow the road down then round and up to the right passing Lodge Farm. The road bends distinctly to the right passing a cluster of houses and passes between two stone gateposts, after which turn right along a track towards Home Farm. Head straight on passing the farm to your right along a grassy track and follow this old lane up to the left up into Aislaby.

Perched high on a hillside and far away from the tourist trail, Aislaby stands proud above the surrounding countryside with unsurpassed views of the broad acres of Esk Dale, Sleights and the secretive Little Beck Valley. First settled by the Danes over 1,000 years ago, this was where Asulf had his farm.

The village of today has a real mixture of buildings with some fine old houses, in particular the rather eccentric Pond House. Once a centre for quarrying, the Aislaby Quarries to the west of the village are now redundant; however, in years gone by stone was extracted from here of such durability that many of our sea defences, pier supports and even London Bridge was constructed using it.

Turn right along the road through the village, then as the road leaves the village and bends round to the left turn right along the track known as Featherbed Lane. After 200 yards turn to the right along a narrow paved path that leads steeply down the hillside to reach the main road.

A network of ancient paved paths, or trods, once connected important trading centres in medieval times and were used up until the 19th century primarily by packhorses to transport a variety of goods such as coal and fish, although some of these trods have monastic or even prehistoric origins. The delightfully named Featherbed Lane is a pleasure to walk on, but take care when the stones are wet, as they can be very slippery.

Cross over the road and head along the track opposite, passing to the left of the water pumping station where a

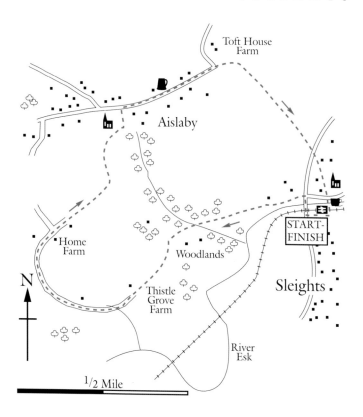

paved path again leads down to reach the Ruswarp Road –
River Gardens Café is a short distance to the left. At the
road turn right then cross the footbridge to the left over the
Esk that leads across the railway line near Sleights Station,
(take care crossing the railway line) and onto a road, which
you follow to the right back up to the parking area.

EAST ROW TEA ROOM

S A N D S E N D

A bracing cliff-top walk with stunning views of Whitby Abbey in the distance with an easy stroll along the disused coastal railway line.

TEA SHOP
East Row Tea Room
Estbek House Hotel
East Row
Sandsend
Tel: 01947 893424
OPEN:
Every day, all year.
MAP:
OS Outdoor Leisure
Map 27
DISTANCE
3 miles (4.8 km)
ALLOW:
1¹/₂ hours
PARKING:
Large pay and display car park at the foot of Lythe Bank in Sandsend.

Sandsend is essentially two settlements with East Row built around East Row Beck as well as along the sea front and Sandsend proper along the banks of Sandsend Beck, also known as Mickleby Beck. Old stone cottages face each other across these streams as if they wished they were part of a moorland village rather than a seaside resort. As the name suggests, Sandsend lies at the end of the long sweep of beach from Whitby, a rarity along this part of the coast, and has an air of dignity about it; Sandsend has not sold its soul to tourism. The village has a long tradition of industry dating back to the Romans who had a cement works here and later in the 17th century alum was mined along the coast at Sandsend Ness. Used in the tanning process as well as to fix dyes, alum was a very valuable commodity, the production of which was once a papal secret. The last alum mine closed in 1871 as cheaper production methods were discovered; however, the coast is still severely scarred. Mulgrave Wood stretches inland from Sandsend for over four miles in which the home of the Marquis of Normanby lies hidden away, a grand 18th century house where famous guests such as Wordsworth and Dickens once stayed. In the heart of this ancient deciduous woodland are the remains of the earlier Mulgrave Castle dating from the 13th century as well as the even older 11th century Foss Castle, said to have been the home of the legendary giant known as Wade who also supposedly built Wade's Causeway, the Roman Road that stretches across moorland near the village of Goathland.

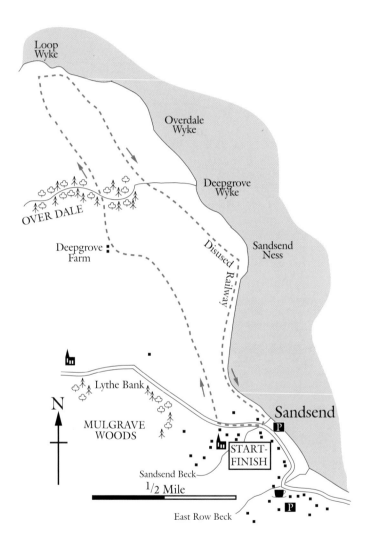

Loop Wyke

Overdale Wyke

Deepgrove Wyke

OVER DALE

Deepgrove Farm

Disused Railway

Sandsend Ness

Lythe Bank

N

MULGRAVE WOODS

Sandsend

P

START-FINISH

Sandsend Beck

1/2 Mile

East Row Beck

P

From the bridge over Sandsend Beck follow the main road steeply up Lythe bank out of the village, with views of the attractive assortment of cottages alongside Sandsend Beck to your left – note the old parapets of the railway viaduct across the stream as well as the station at the top of the bank up to your right. Follow the road steeply up then at the bench just before the North York Moors National Park sign follow the footpath to the right through a kissing gate with superb views of the sweeping bay and Whitby Abbey in the distance.

The path heads straight on alongside a fence on your left for a short distance then along a fence on your right up to the top of the bank, at the top of which bear left across the field keeping close to the fence on your right. As you approach a fence across your path bear up to the left away from the sea to a stile in the far corner of the field. After the stile veer slightly to the left across the field, marked by posts, to reach a stile by a gate. Follow the clear grassy track ahead as it winds its way to reach Deepgrove Farm. Immediately before the farm buildings turn right, marked 'Kettleness', and head straight on across the field, through a gate then alongside the fence and hedge on your left and into woodland. The path now drops steeply down steps into the confines of Over Dale, crosses a footbridge then climbs steeply up again to reach a stile. After the stile head along the hedge on your left until you come to the cliffs above the North Sea.

What a wonderful view from this breezy height over 300 feet above sea level with plunging cliffs, white-water breakers and the endless sea complete with distant boats on the horizon. Thankfully this stunning coastal scenery is protected as part of

North Yorkshire's Heritage Coast.

Turn right and follow the clear coastal path; Whitby soon comes into view with the famous Abbey and harbour wall clearly visible. After a short distance the path leaves the cliff top and bends to the right to run along the top of the field with the cliffs and sea away to your left to reach a stile that leads into woodland – this clearly marked path has been diverted to avoid erosion to the cliff top. A very steep path heads down steps once again into Over Dale to reach the old railway line.

This is the old trackbed of the Whitby to Middlesbrough line via Loftus and the coast, built in 1883. Once one of the most scenic railway journeys in England, the line was difficult to maintain due to coastal erosion and was closed in 1958, although the section from Middlebrough to Saltburn remains open to passengers with a freight line continuing to Boulby to service its Potash Mine. The boarded up tunnel stretches for over a mile to re-emerge near Kettleness and stands as a tribute to the skill of its Victorian engineers.

Follow the old railway line to the left along the coast for one mile back to Sandsend, passing the distinctive outcrop of Sandsend Ness and the scarred landscape of the alum mining industry. As you reach Sandsend the path drops down to the left through the parking area to reach the starting point at the foot of Lythe Bank.

SHEPHERD'S PURSE

The unmistakable landmark of the ruins of Whitby Abbey silhouetted against the sky provides a spiritual companion for this exhilarating coastal walk.

TEA SHOP
Shepherd's Purse
Church Street
Whitby
Tel: 01947 820228
OPEN:
All day, every day
MAP:
OS Outdoor Leisure
Map 27
DISTANCE:
4½ miles (7.2 km)
ALLOW:
2 hours
PARKING:
Several car parks to
choose from

Whitby has an air of adventure and excitement about it that adds to the sense of anticipation as you enter the town. Perhaps it is the fact that the only approach is across bleak moorland roads and your first view is one of a jumble of houses fighting for space along the steep cliffs and valley sides with the rolling ocean stretching out to the horizon. This bustling town is still a working port, but during the 18th and 19th centuries it was one of England's most important seaports with shipbuilding, fishing, whaling, alum and jet industries providing employment. 200 years ago whaling ships regularly set sail from here for the inhospitable Arctic waters, the whale blubber being rendered on the quayside into oil which was then used as fuel for the town's streetlights, as well as being sold for other uses further afield. The famous explorer Captain James Cook set sail from here on his voyages of discovery in his Whitby-built ship, the *Endeavour*.

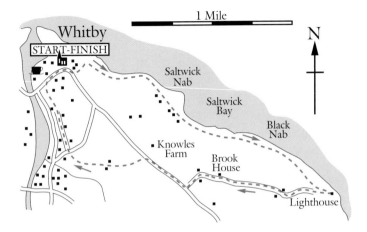

From the centre of Whitby cross the swing bridge over the harbour heading towards the Abbey along Bridge Street then, as the road bends round to the right, turn to your left along Church Street, marked 'Whitby Abbey'. Follow this cobbled street through the heart of old Whitby and then round to the right to the bottom of the famous 199 steps that lead up to St Mary's Church.

From here you get a superb bird's eye view of the town, its dramatic setting at the mouth of the Esk shown to good effect with boats, yachts and trawlers safely moored in the harbour. Beneath your feet lies the heart of the fishing village of Whitby with old cottages crowding together for protection against the fierce winds that blow off the North Sea.

Climb up the steps then, after catching your breath, follow the path straight on passing the church and then head along the road between the Abbey ruins and the Coastguard Station. At the end of the buildings on your left turn to your left into Abbey Farm and head through the farmyard to join the spectacular cliff-top path. Follow this path to the right to reach the caravan site near to the promontory of Saltwick Bay, which is now in the care of the National Trust. Follow the clear wide path that bears to the right up through the holiday park to reach a stile at the end of the park that leads on to the cliff-top path once again (signpost 'Cleveland Way'), with the sandy expanses of Saltwick Bay down to your left.

The clear path continues straight on climbing steadily up to reach the old Fog Signal Station. Standing over 300 feet above sea level with expansive vistas out to sea the now redundant fog horn, known as the Hawsker Bull, was last sounded in 1988.

Continue along the coastal path until you reach the

Lighthouse, immediately before which head up to the right to join the road. Turn right and follow this quiet winding country lane for almost a mile, passing through the farmyard of Brook House, to reach the main road. Turn right along the road heading towards Whitby Abbey in the distance and passing the entrance to the holiday park.

Just after the turning for Knowles Farm take the path to the left through the gap in the wall and follow the path down alongside the hedge, complete with a line of telegraph poles, to reach a group of farm buildings and a road. Continue straight on along the road then as the road bends to the right head straight on along a paved path to the left of the houses which brings you out on a road in the suburbs of Whitby. Cross the road and follow The Ropery opposite at the end of which a path winds its way above the rooftops of Whitby back to Whitby Abbey and St Mary's Church where you retrace your steps back into the historic quarter of Whitby.

Whitby Abbey, or Streonshalh as it was known then, was founded in 657AD by St Hilda. However, this early seat of Christianity was destroyed by invading Danes in the 9th century; the present abbey dates from the 11th century, although much building work took place in the 13th century. It was here in 664 that the Synod of Whitby decided to follow Roman Catholic rather than Celtic Christianity and also decided upon the dates of Easter. Whitby Abbey was the home of Caedmon who wrote the first poem in English in the 7th century; a beautifully carved cross stands in the churchyard in his memory. The 12th century Church of St Mary is famous for its interior which was fitted out by local craftsmen more used to building ships and so has a rather nautical feel. This windswept churchyard provided the inspiration for Bram Stoker's Dracula.

BRAMBLEWICK TEA ROOMS

If you undertake this walk at dusk you may catch sight of smugglers moving their contraband under cover of darkness or even a mischievous hobgoblin hiding in its cave.

TEA SHOP
Bramblewick Tea
Rooms, The Dock
Robin Hood's Bay
Tel: 01947 880418
OPEN:
Every day from Easter
until end Oct, week-
ends during winter.
MAP:
OS Outdoor Leisure
Map 27
DISTANCE:
5 miles (8 km)
ALLOW:2¹/₂ hours
PARKING:
Pay and display car
parks in centre of
village.

Considered by many to be the prettiest fishing village on the Yorkshire coast, Robin Hood's Bay, or simply 'Bay' if you are local, clings precariously to steep cliffs, its tiny cottages with their distinctive red pantile roofs crowding around the ravine of King's Beck for protection against the fierce winds that blow in from the North Sea. The day I visited the village a strong wind whipped up a high tide sending waves crashing up the main street as far as the tea room's door, which reminded me of the story of a ship whose bowsprit smashed the window of a pub! This stretch of coastline is notorious for its storms; indeed in 1780 the main King Street was washed away taking some cottages with it, and many more houses have been lost to the sea since. A sea wall was built in 1975 which keeps the worst of the waves at bay; however, it is only a temporary measure as the relentless erosive action of the waves is eating away at the surrounding cliffs at a rate of five centimetres every year. Robin Hood's Bay has been an important fishing village since the 1500s with over 130 families living off the sea during the 1830s. Once a haunt of smugglers, it was said that their illegal contraband of rum, brandy and tobacco could be moved through the village via a maze of tunnels and secret passages without ever seeing the light of day. A handful of traditional fishing boats, or cobles, are still launched along the slipway quite literally at the end of the main street in the heart of the old village. This very steep road was built to replace King Street and links up the old village with the more modern development at the top of the bank, which grew steadily after the railway arrived in 1885 and was also where the more prosperous sea captains built their houses.

From the car parks above the old village, follow the steep road down into the heart of Robin Hood's Bay until you reach the slipway and the end of the road. Follow the steps to the right up Covet Hill that lead onto the promenade, then head along the path that climbs up the hillside to the right, with wooden steps in places, to reach the cliff-top path. A clear paved path follows the cliff edge all the way to the picturesque inlet known as Boggle Hole.

The path drops steeply down steps into the confines of the ravine, across a footbridge over Mill Beck beside the Youth Hostel, then climbs up more steps and onto a road. Turn right along this road then immediately turn to

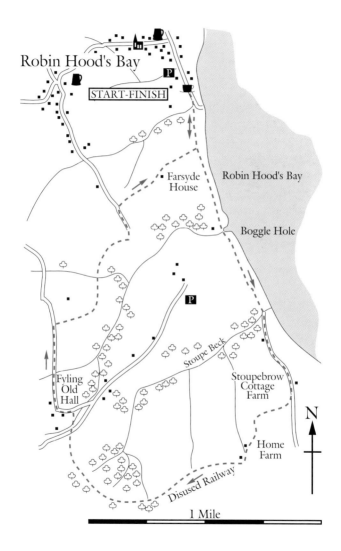

Robin Hood's Bay

START-FINISH

Farsyde House

Robin Hood's Bay

Boggle Hole

Stoupe Beck

Stoupebrow Cottage Farm

Fyling Old Hall

Home Farm

N

Disused Railway

1 Mile

your left, marked 'Cleveland Way', and follow the steps steeply once again to the top of the cliffs with superb retrospective views of Robin Hood's Bay.

A Boggle is the local name for a hobgoblin, the mischievous 'little people' that were thought to live in caves along the coast as well as the more remote corners of the Moors. Boggle Hole was where smugglers used to land their contraband. This cliff-top path affords superb views of Robin Hood's Bay, which sweeps in a graceful curve from the promontory of North Cheek, also called Ness Point, to South Cheek or The Old Peak. At low tide bands of soft shale and hard limestone are revealed to spectacular effect in the shape of curving ridges. The haunt of geologists and fossil hunters, this rocky foreshore is a fascinating place to explore but keep a careful eye on the rising tide.

Continue along the cliff-edge path, which soon leads down into the next ravine of Stoupe Beck, over a footbridge and then up to the right along a track to reach Stoupe Bank Farm. Follow the road passing the farm and then after passing the next group of buildings at Stoupe Brow Cottage Farm take the track to the right. Follow this track straight on then turn left over a stile, marked by a signpost, and head uphill keeping close to the hedge on your left and over another stile in a fence to the left of Home Farm. After this stile bear to the right up across the field to reach a stile by a gate at the top of the field which leads onto the old railway line. Turn right and follow the old trackbed as it gently curves round to the right for one mile until it drops down to reach a road.

Opened in 1885, this stretch of line from Scarborough to Whitby was one of the most dramatic routes in England with

superb coastal scenery all the way; unfortunately this was not a consideration when Beeching wielded his infamous axe in 1965. Today the old trackbed is now used as a footpath providing an easy route through some beautiful countryside with deep wooded ravines and old railway bridges combining to make a fascinating walk.

At the road turn left and follow it up bearing round to the right at the elegant Fyling Hall after which continue along the road for almost half a mile. Just before you come to the hill with a gradient of one-in-five, turn to your right along a track, marked by a signpost, and follow it down over the old railway line again and through some gates. After the second gate follow the path to the left alongside a fence, paved in places, which drops down into the confines of Mill Beck. Cross the footbridge over the stream then head up across the field bearing to the right to reach the top of the bank.

Turn right along the now level path keeping close to the hedge on your left to join the road. Follow the road to the left then after a short distance turn right along Mark Lane towards Farsyde Stud. As you approach Farsyde House take the well-marked path to the left that skirts around the buildings to join the cliff-top path again, where you turn left and retrace your steps back into Robin Hood's Bay.

There are several theories as to why this little fishing village should be named after the famous outlaw, one of the most common is that Robin Hood fled here to escape capture and disguised himself as a fisherman.

PRUDOM HOUSE TEA ROOMS

A short walk incorporating two of the area's finest waterfalls and the legend of the path built by a giant.

TEA SHOP
Prudom House Tea
Rooms
Goathland
Tel: 01947 896368
OPEN:
Every day from mid
Feb until end Oct.
MAP:
OS Outdoor Leisure
Map 27
DISTANCE:
4 miles (6.4 km)
ALLOW:
2 hours
PARKING:
Pay and display car
park at Goathland.

Goathland will be instantly recognisable to millions of people as 'Aidensfield' from the TV series *Heartbeat*, which means that on a sunny weekend the car parks fill up very early. Television fame aside, Goathland has been attracting tourists for well over 100 years who come here to soak up its unique atmosphere. This dispersed moorland village is situated over 500 feet above sea level along a ridge above the deep ravines of West Beck and Eller Beck. Between the houses and the road is a rambling green where sheep graze freely, although they seem to prefer to sit in the road most of the time! There is some confusion as to the origins of the name of the village, but what is certain is that it has nothing to do with goats! It is most probably derived from an old Scandinavian personal name; however, some historians claim that it means 'God's Land' as a hermitage dedicated to St Mary was established here in the 12th century. Nothing is left of this early religious site and the present church dates from 1896. The attention to detail at Goathland Station is excellent offering a glimpse of the 'golden age of steam' and making it a popular stop on the North Yorkshire Moors Railway that runs from Grosmont to Pickering. The railway opened in 1836 bringing early tourists to this area, hence the large Victorian hotels and houses; the line fell victim to Beeching's axe in 1965.

Leave Goathland along the footpath that passes to the right of the Mallyan Spout Hotel, opposite the church, and follow the clear path down to West Beck. Turn left along the riverbank, over slippery rocks and boulders, to reach the slender waterfall of Mallyan Spout.

There is a distinct lack of waterfalls in the North York Moors due to the underlying rocks and lack of rainfall. So a waterfall with a graceful 70-foot drop, the highest in the Moors, over moss and fern covered rocks in a beautiful setting is an understandably popular tourist 'honey pot'; just pick your time carefully to avoid the crowds.

Continue to follow the clearly marked path along the side of the stream for three quarters of a mile to reach the road bridge. This walk along the banks of West Beck, a tributary of the River Esk, is an absolute delight with ancient woodland, overhanging crags and the playful river keeping you company.

At the road turn left and follow it up sharply round to the left then take the track to the right passing New Wath

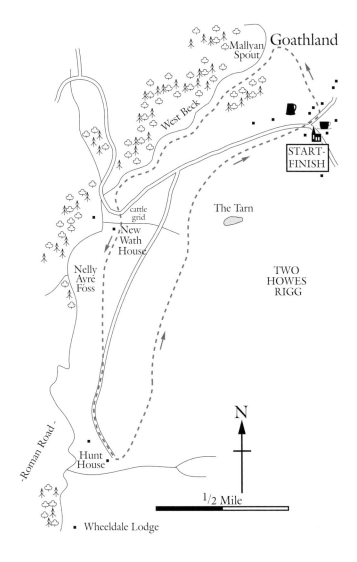

Goathland

Mallyan
Spout

West Beck

START-
FINISH

cattle
grid

The Tarn

New
Wath
House

Nelly
Ayre
Foss

TWO
HOWES
RIGG

N

Roman Road

Hunt
House

1/2 Mile

Wheeldale Lodge

House, marked 'Nelly Ayre Foss'. Continue along the grassy path alongside the stone wall on your right until you eventually reach the end of the wall and a signpost.

Nelly Ayre Foss is well worth the short diversion down to the right, with the waters of Wheeldale Beck plunging over rock ledges in a sylvan setting.

At the signpost bear up across the moor to the left to join the road where you turn right and follow it to reach Hunt House.

England's best-preserved stretch of Roman Road can be seen on the hillside to the right. Known as Wade's Causeway, this Roman Road stretches for over a mile across Wheeldale Moor and stands over 16 feet wide paved with large blocks of stone,

although it originally would have also had a gravel surface. Dating from the first century AD this road was built to provide the Roman legions with quick and easy access to quell the troublesome Brigantes tribes and ran from York via Malton to Esk Dale and possibly a coastal signal station. Some historians doubt its Roman origins and believe it may even pre-date the Roman occupation. Folklore would have us believe that it was constructed by a giant called Wade as a footpath for his wife to make her journey to market easier.

As you pass Hunt House, take the bridleway to the left immediately before the road crosses a small stream and becomes a rougher track. Follow this path to the left back on yourself across rough moorland – there are several paths to choose from – and head for the top of the ridge to reach a cairn to the right of a solitary tree. At the top of the ridge flat moorland stretches out before you; pick up a clear path that skirts to the left along the edge of the ridge with a drop to the left down to the valley of Wheeldale Beck. A boggy and stony path, marked by a series of cairns, follows the edge of the moor offering fantastic views. After about half a mile you come to a junction of paths with one heading straight on downhill and the other path bending away to the right towards The Tarn – our path heads straight on downhill along a sunken path. The path soon levels out and crosses an area of boggy ground then continues on gradually bending round to the right to eventually join the road at Goathland near to the Pinfold.

These small circular stone enclosures were used to pen stray animals until their owners paid a small fine; this pinfold was still in use up until the 1920s.

HACKNESS GRANGE

HACKNESS

A journey through dales that are so deep they never see the sun's rays during the winter months.

TEA SHOP
Hackness Grange
Country House
Hackness
Nr Scarborough
Tel: 01723 882345
OPEN:
All day, every day
MAP:
OS Outdoor Leisure
Map 27
DISTANCE:
5 miles (8 km)
ALLOW:
2 hours
PARKING:
Hacknesss Grange
car park, ask
permission first.
Also limited parking
in the centre of the
village opposite the
school

This attractive village lies hidden amongst the numerous valleys that cut deep into the surrounding moorland, a tranquil haven away from the hustle and bustle of Scarborough which, unbelievably, is only three miles away. Dominating the village is the 18th century Hackness Hall, home of Lord Derwent. It was designed by John Carr, who also designed Harewood House, and replaced an Elizabethan manor house which was unceremoniously pulled down to improve the views across the lake from the new house. The lake was originally the fishpond of a nunnery established here in 680AD by St Hilda of Whitby Abbey, the remains of which are probably submerged beneath the lake which was enlarged when the Hall was built. This early religious site was attacked by Danes in the 9th century; however, a Benedictine monastery was established here again in the late 11th century following the Norman Conquest

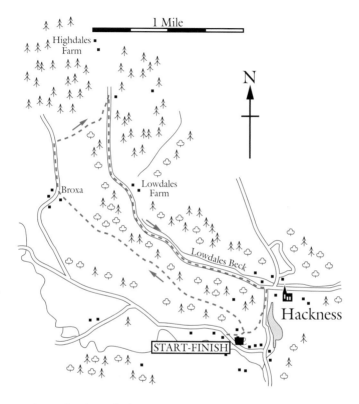

and survived until the Dissolution of the Monasteries. Adjacent to the Hall stands the beautiful old Church of St Peter, originally dedicated to St Mary, which dates from 1050 and still boasts many original features despite later additions, particularly during the 11th-13th centuries. Inside the church are the fragments of a Saxon Cross that once stood in the nunnery to a height of fifteen feet, and is thought to date from 720AD.

From the car park at Hackness Grange follow the right-hand access road back onto the main road, then turn left and almost immediately take the track off to the right and follow this up, passing Keepers Cottage, into woodland to reach a junction of tracks. Follow the track up to the left to reach a gate, after which the track levels out and exits the wood.

Continue straight on keeping close to the fence and woodland on your left, then as you approach the wall across your path bear to the right across the field and through a gate in the wall. After this gate walk straight on alongside the wood and ridge on your right keeping to the perimeter of the field, over several stiles until you reach the last field before the hamlet of Broxa. Bear up to the left across this last field towards the farmhouse and go through the gate in the hedge that leads onto a lane to the right of the farm buildings.

There are numerous steep-sided valleys in this area that have cut so deep into the moorland that some slopes do not see any sunlight throughout the winter months. Our walk along Broxa Rigg affords superb views through the trees down into Low Dales, whilst the walk from Broxa along the road offers far-reaching vistas across the valley of the River Derwent. These valleys are a haven for birdwatchers, and many have attractive names such as Trouts Dale, Bee Dale and Whisper Dales – there is no need to talk in hushed tones in this valley as its name is derived from White Spot Dale.

Head straight on along the lane passing the farm on your left then bear round to the right out of the hamlet. Continue along the lane for about a quarter of a mile then take the footpath to the right through a gate in the

hedge just after the last telegraph pole in the hedge. Head straight across the field and over a stile in the fence that leads into woodland. A clear path drops steeply down through the woods to reach a fence at the bottom of the hill; turn right here along the fence for a short distance then take the stile to the left over the fence that leads onto open fields.

Walk straight across the field through two successive gaps in the hedge, then head alongside the fence to join a clear track. Just after the gate a clearly marked path heads to the right over a stile then drops down over Highdales Beck and up to join a track immediately below a house. Turn right along this track, through a gate, then continue along the road heading down sylvan High Dales to reach the attractive group of houses at Lowdales. Follow the road round to the right, along the ford/road, and on for a further three-quarters of a mile back in to Hackness. If the ford/road is flooded then follow the path that runs from Lowdales parallel to the road to the left.

This has to be one of the longest fords in the country. Most of the year it is perfectly dry as Lowdales Beck flows beneath the road. However after heavy rain the road is transformed into a river for almost 400 yards.

When you reach the road junction at Hackness turn right along the main road then, with the small lake to your left, take the track that branches off to the right. Follow this track up through a gate then where the track splits take the left-hand branch and retrace your steps back to the car park.

BALDERSON'S WELCOME CAFÉ

THORNTON-LE-DALE

A pleasant walk incorporating the fine Anglo-Saxon church of St Hilda as well as the evocatively named Howl Dale, a remnant of a Royal hunting forest.

TEA SHOP
Balderson's Welcome Café, Thornton-le-Dale, Pickering
Tel: 01751 474272
OPEN:
Every day Feb – mid Nov, closed mid Nov – end Jan.
MAP:
OS Outdoor Leisure Map 27
DISTANCE:
5¹/₂ miles (8.8 km)
ALLOW: 2¹/₂ hours
PARKING:
Large National Park pay and display car park

Thornton-le-Dale, sometimes spelt without the 'le' although I much prefer its more formal 'Sunday' name, is an exceptionally attractive village, so much so that it was awarded the 'Best Kept Village Trophy 1999, Rural Community Council'. Old stone-built cottages line its streets, some of which date back to the 14th century and are of cruck-frame construction. Of particular note are the 17th century Lady Lumley's Almshouses, a wonderful row of twelve tiny cottages built for the poor people of the district and still used for their original purpose. Thornton Beck, complete with noisy ducks, meanders through the heart of the village and is spanned by numerous bridges; the view along the beck towards the thatched Beck Isle Cottage is one of England's most photographed scenes. Mentioned in the Domesday Book, Thornton-le-Dale was first settled over 1,000

years ago and grew in importance as a trading centre,
gaining its market charter in 1281. On the small green in
the centre of the village stands the weathered market
cross as well as the 19th century stocks for the more
unruly inhabitants.

From the village green at the centre of Thornton-le-Dale
walk along the main road towards Scarborough passing
Lady Lumley's Almshouses. At the road bridge across
Thornton Beck turn left along the footpath which runs
along the left bank of the beck, passing the thatched Beck
Isle Cottage, until you reach a road. Turn left along the
road and follow it up to Thornton Mill.

*The waters of Thornton Beck once provided power for a
thriving mill industry with commodities such as wool, flour,
paper and cloth being processed.*

Just before the road crosses the beck at the mill buildings,
turn right, marked by a signpost, and follow the path
passing to the right of the mill and warehouse, after
which cross over a stile and bear left through an area of
conifers to run alongside the beck. Follow this pleasant
riverside path all the way to Low Farm; the path joins
the farm track to the left of the farm buildings, which
you follow to the left to reach Ellerburn Church.

*This hidden church dedicated to St Hilda is an ecclesiastical
gem; it exudes the spirit of early Christian worship in this
country. The present church dates from the mid 11th century,
although it stands on the site of a much earlier wooden church
destroyed by marauding Danes during the Dark Ages. Built
into its walls are a wealth of Anglo-Saxon and Viking cross*

*heads and carvings from this original church. Spend time
exploring and you will be richly rewarded.*

Our path heads along the grassy track to the left of the
church. Follow this track up across arable land keeping
close to the wall on your right to reach a gate that leads
into woodland, then continue along the clear track up
through the woods to reach the road. Just off the track to
the left in the woods are ditches that once formed part of
a defensive system built by Brigantes tribes – the
'Private' signs relate to the surrounding woodland not the
track.

At the road turn left, then at the road junction turn left
again along the main road, taking care of traffic. After
approximately a quarter of a mile turn off the road to the
right along a track marked by a 'Dead End' sign and

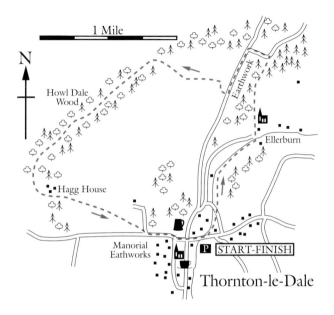

follow it round to the right, then take the wide path to
the left, marked by a signpost. Follow this track alongside
the stone wall on your right then drop down the hillside
through woodland to the valley floor of Howl Dale. Turn
left and follow the track through Howl Dale.

*Evocatively named Howl Dale has an eerie atmosphere,
particularly at dusk. A relic of the once important hunting
forest of the Royal Forest of Pickering, Howl Dale still has
many mature deciduous trees on one side of the valley
although conifers cloak the other, all of which provides a
variety of habitats for a profusion of birds.*

At the end of the woods a wide path bears round to the
left and up to reach a gate then continues straight on

through a series of gates passing to the right of Hagg House Farm and onto a farm road. Cross over the road and follow the footpath slightly to the left over a stile and up through woodland then out across open fields, with expansive views of the Vale of Pickering opening up. The path heads alongside the hedge on your left then joins a track which you follow down to the right for a short distance. A path turns off this track to the left over a stile near to a clump of trees, after which a clear path heads straight on across fields, gradually bearing down to the right to join the road at the edge of Thornton-le-Dale.

As you join the road note the earthworks in the field opposite. These are the only remains of Roxby Castle, one time home of Sir Richard Cholmley, the 'Great Black Knight of the North' who served at the court of Elizabeth I and lies buried in the churchyard at Thornton-le-Dale. Another 'resident' of All Saints churchyard is Matthew Grimes who helped guard Napoleon on the island of St Helena.

MULBERRIES COFFEE SHOP

P I C K E R I N G

A walk through the Royal hunting preserve of the Forest of Pickering.

TEA SHOP
Mulberries Coffee Shop
Bridge Street
Pickering
Tel: 01751 472337
OPEN:
Open every day all year
MAP:
OS Outdoor Leisure Map 27
DISTANCE:
5 miles (8 km)
ALLOW:
2 hours.
PARKING:
Pay and display parking in the town centre.

According to legend Pickering was founded in 270BC by the British King Pereduras, who named the town after he found his mislaid ring inside a pike which had been cooked for his dinner! Pickering Castle is a superb example of a motte and bailey castle and dates from Norman times when William the Conqueror ordered a wooden structure to be built to control the unruly North. Although its walls were later rebuilt in stone, the castle saw little military action and developed primarily as a Royal hunting lodge for Medieval Kings to hunt in the nearby Forest of Pickering. The Castle passed into the ownership of John o' Gaunt in 1346 who was created Duke of Lancaster – his son became King Henry V and title and manor have remained with the Sovereign to this day. Pickering has been an important trading centre for

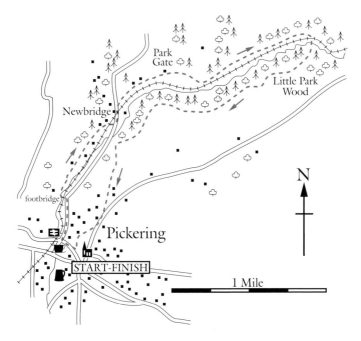

centuries and was famous for the manufacture of red roof tiles, known as pantiles, as well as a centre for the breeding of coach horses, mainly dales bred Cleveland Bays; the London General Omnibus Co., State coaches, the Royal Family and even the King of Italy used these horses. Pickering has matured into an attractive country town with a relaxed pace of life. Fascinating old shops and inns line its busy streets, narrow alleys and lanes; spend some time exploring and you will be richly rewarded.

From the centre of Pickering head out of the town along Park Street passing the railway station on your left. After the old mill buildings turn left, marked by a car parking sign, over the level crossing (take care) then almost straight away turn to the right along the second turning to pass to the left of the Fishing Lake Café where a footbridge takes you on to a riverside walk.

Cross over the stile to the left at the end of this riverside path, after which turn right along the grassy track to reach a gate that leads onto a stony track. Head straight on along this track with the railway line to your right, passing through the front yard of a house, after which continue on through a series of gates to reach a road at the group of houses at Newbridge. The footpath turns off the road immediately before the houses and crosses the railway line (take care) and Pickering Beck to reach the road.

The North Yorkshire Moors Railway keeps you company for the first half of this walk and provides a constant source of fascination along the way with particular highlights being the elegant stone built Pickering Station, which dates from 1845 and the advent of steam trains, the Newbridge level crossing and the picturesque railway line through sylvan Newton Dale. Keep a camera handy for when a steam train chuffs its way along the valley.

Turn left along the road, over the level crossing then take the first turning on the right opposite the entrance to Newbridge Quarry and follow this lane for half a mile to reach the farm buildings of Park Gate where the road becomes a rough track. Head straight on along the track into the 'Duchy of Lancaster Pickering Woods', and follow the track as it meanders through woodland then drops down alongside the railway line.

The ancient hunting preserve of the Forest of Pickering became Crown property centuries ago and is still owned by the Queen through the Duchy of Lancaster. Today the forest is managed on a commercial basis for timber and game shooting; if you are quiet you may be lucky enough to catch a glimpse of deer in the woods as well as more common game such as grouse, pheasant and rabbits.

As the track bends slightly away from the railway line take the track again marked by a 'Duchy of Lancaster' sign and follow this very rocky track alongside the railway line for approximately three-quarters of a mile. As the railway line begins to bend gradually to the right, turn off the track to the right along a path across the

railway line by way of a stile (take care) – this stile is hidden in undergrowth and is marked by a marker-post at the side of the track; take care crossing the track. After the railway line, the path crosses a footbridge over Pickering Beck then splits; our route follows the left-hand branch which meanders up to join a rough track across your path. Turn right along this track then almost immediately follow the track to your left that leads very steeply uphill alongside an old wall, over another track, until you reach the top of the hill. At the top of the hill turn right along the footpath which runs parallel to and is slightly higher than the track to the right; this path heads through the woods to reach a kissing gate at the end of the woods. The path now heads straight on for over a mile through a series of kissing gates across fields keeping close to the field boundary on your right.

You eventually come to a small wooden gate in the fence on your right; turn left here bearing up across the field to reach a stile in an overgrown hedge directly underneath a line of tall poplar trees. After the stile head straight on along the track known as Love Lane, which soon becomes very clear and leads back in to Pickering along the Whitby Road.

As you walk back in to Pickering take time to look round the church of St Peter and St Paul, which houses some of the best examples of 15th century frescoes in the country. These wall paintings had been hidden since the Reformation underneath layers of whitewash until they were 'discovered' in 1851, only to be covered over again until 1878 by the vicar who feared idolatrous parishioners.

MUCKY DUCK INN

N E W T O N - O N - R A W C L I F F E

The screech of the steam train's whistle echoes along the glacial gorge of Newton Dale.

TEA SHOP
Mucky Duck Inn,
Newton-on-Rawcliffe,
Pickering
Tel: 01751 472505
OPEN:
Every day, all year
MAP:
OS Outdoor Leisure
Map 27
DISTANCE:
6 miles (9.6 km)
ALLOW:
3 hours
PARKING:
On-street parking in
the village

The focal point of Newton-on-Rawcliffe is its village pond complete with noisy ducks! A relic of the days when most of the villages in this area had ponds to compensate for the lack of plentiful local water supplies due to the underlying pervious limestone rock strata of the Tabular Hills. It is a classic linear village with an assortment of attractive houses lining a spacious green.

Head along the road up through the village then as you leave the

93

village behind take the track immediately to the right,
marked 'Link Levisham', and follow this often very muddy
track down until views of Newton Dale open up to your
left.

*This is one of the finest views in the North York Moors with a
superb panorama across the deep wooded gorge of Newton Dale
along the bottom of which runs the sinuous trackbed of the North
Yorkshire Moors Railway. The Newtondale Gorge was scoured
out by the powerful erosive force of glacial melt waters at the end
of the last Ice Age. You are also standing on the edge of the vast
Cropton Forest, first planted in the 1920s and one of the largest
commercial forests in the country. Often criticised due to the
regimental rows of single species trees, this forest has now
matured adding a new dimension to the Moors landscape as well
as providing recreational facilities and, more importantly,
employment.*

As soon as the view has opened out of Newton Dale, turn
immediately to the left over a stile, marked by a signpost,
bearing right at the bench along a very steep and muddy
path down Newton Banks until you reach a gate and stile.
Do not head through this gate but turn back on yourself
and head across the field (no clear path) towards the far
bottom corner of the field with Levisham Station in the
distance. You soon pick up a clearer path that heads steeply
down through woods, over a footbridge across Pickering
Beck and along the road to reach Levisham Station.

*What a wonderful place! You really do feel as though you have
stepped back in time with well-maintained cottages, signal box,
rolling stock and station, complete with old-fashioned ticket office,
adding to the turn-of-the-century atmosphere. One of the first
passenger railways in the world, this line was designed by George*

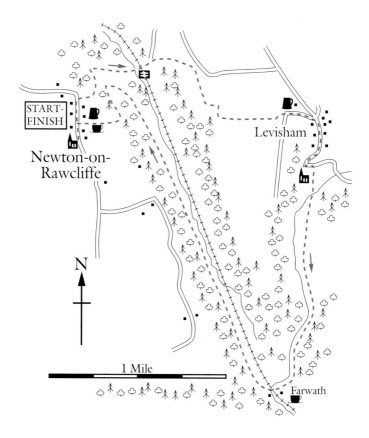

Stephenson and completed in 1836. The section between Grosmont and Pickering was controversially closed by Beeching in 1965 but reopened again in 1973 as the North Yorkshire Moors Railway, a preserved railway run by very professional enthusiasts. The blast of the steam train's whistle echoing down the valley is an evocative and exciting sound.

Walk over the level crossing and follow the road up over a cattle grid, then take the path to the right over a stream and through a gate immediately after the house on the right. Follow the path up through the woods and through a gate that brings you out on the open hillside, then head straight uphill to reach a stile next to a gate. Cross the stile and turn right along the grassy track that gradually climbs up the hillside then bends round to the left and levels out along the top of a steep bank to your right, with incredible views across the valley. The path now turns and heads steeply down to the right traversing the side valley along a narrow path that runs above a wood to reach a stile. Cross the stile then turn left alongside the wall which soon joins a road that leads into Levisham.

Perched high on the edge of the gently rising Levisham Moor, the village of Levisham is almost an exact replica of Newton-on-Rawcliffe, apart from the pond, and was first settled in pre-Conquest days by a Saxon called Leofgeat's who built his homestead here, hence the name of the village. Levisham's main claim to fame is the fact that it can only be reached via tortuously steep roads that snake up the sides of the steep gorges of Newton Dale and Levisham Beck.

Turn right and follow the road through the village, at the end of which continue to follow the road that bends very steeply downhill and round to the left, where you turn right along a stony track, marked by a signpost. Where the track forks, follow the left-hand branch that leads to the sad ruins of St Mary's Church.

A place of worship for 1,000 years, the roofless remains and crumbling tower of St Mary' Church have a sad and forlorn atmosphere, and contrast with its beautiful and peaceful

*surroundings; the church has not been used for worship since the
1950s.*

Continue along the track passing the church on your right
then cross the footbridge over Levisham Beck and follow
the path up through a gate and on to join a very clear
broad track. Turn right and follow this track, known as
Sleights Road, down along the side of the valley with the
sparkling waters of Levisham Beck to your right. After one
mile the track bends to the right and crosses a bridge to
reach the small cluster of houses at Farwath, an isolated
spot indeed in a wonderful setting.

Cross the railway line (take care) and then bear right over a
footbridge next to a ford, after which continue along the
track for about 100 yards then turn off to the right along a
clear track, marked by a signpost. Follow this track through
woodland and across meadows for almost two miles – this
is true ancient woodland in its natural state, with deep peat
bogs, wetlands and unimproved grassland.

After two miles the track begins to gradually climb the side
of the hill then, when you are parallel to Levisham Station
down to your right, follow the grassy track up across the
field and round to the left back on yourself to reach a stile
by a gate. Follow the sunken track steeply up through the
woods to reach a level track across your path. Turn right
here then almost immediately take the path to the left over
a stile and back into Newton-on-Rawcliffe.

ABBEY TEA ROOM

An insight into the fascinating industrial legacy of the Rosedale ironstone workings.

TEA SHOP:
Abbey Tea Room,
Rosedale Abbey,
Pickering.
Tel: 01751 417475
OPEN:
Open every day,
except Wed, from
Easter until end Oct.
MAP:
OS Outdoor Leisure
Map 26
DISTANCE:
4 miles (6.4 km)
ALLOW:
2 hours
PARKING:
Free car parks in
centre of village.

Rosedale Abbey lies at the heart of the North York Moors in the beautiful valley of Rosedale. If you are expecting to find the majestic ruins of a great abbey similar to Rievaulx, then you will be disappointed, as all that is left of the Cistercian Priory that gave the village its name is a stone pillar, staircase and sundial. First established in 1158 this small priory was home to nine nuns and a prioress and remained a quiet place of worship until the Dissolution of the Monasteries in 1535. The Priory buildings remained very much intact up until the middle of the 19th century when most of the stones were plundered for building material during the boom years of the local ironstone mines.

From the centre of Rosedale Abbey follow the path that leads between the school and the Church of St Lawrence passing the remains of the priory and onto the road. Cross the road and follow the path directly opposite that leads into the campsite, where you follow the road to the right through the campsite. As you near the end of the site, head along the clearly marked path through a metal gate that leads out into a field.

Walk straight on alongside the hedge on your left across a field, then follow the path down to reach a stile that leads into woodland and a footbridge over the River Seven. Forsake the bridge for the lower path over walkboards along the right-hand bank of the river, cross over a stile then head straight on across the field through a gap in the fence and on to reach a ladder stile.

Continue straight on over the next field, through an overgrown hedge to reach a stile over a fence that leads

onto an often muddy farm track. Turn left down the track, over a small stream and on to reach a gate, after which follow the riverbank until you reach a footbridge. Do not cross the bridge but turn sharp right away from it along the old paved trod up to a stile and small footbridge, after which head up the field, bearing slightly to the right through a gate in the hedge, then continue heading up the field to another gate which leads on to an overgrown track which you follow to reach Hill Cottages and the road.

The rows of cottages perched on the hillside look slightly out of place in this rural landscape. In the mid 19th century the population of Rosedale was almost ten times that of today as the Rosedale ironstone workings were developed to cope with the demand from the expanding heavy industries of Teesside. Ironstone had been mined here since the Iron Age, albeit on a very small scale, and later by the monks of Byland Abbey; however, the rapid development during the Victorian era turned Rosedale into an industrial landscape. It is hard to imagine the amount of industrial activity that once took place here with cottages, workshops, mines, spoil heaps and even a railway.

On the hillside above Hill Cottages are the remains of the calcining kilns and the trackbed of one of the most remarkable railways in England. From here a standard gauge railway was constructed to transport the ironstone to Teesside and operated from 1861 until the mines closed in 1926. This amazing feat of engineering followed the contours of the hills perfectly around the head of Rosedale and Farndale until the final steep descent to join the main line at Battersby Junction via a one-in-five incline. The conspicuous white house was once the home of the manager of the mines.

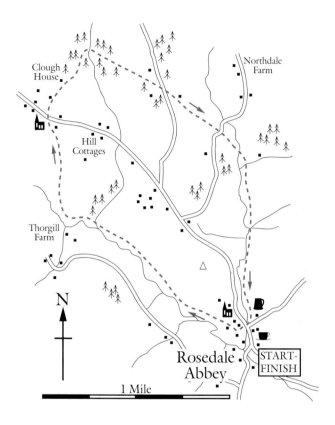

Cross the road and head along the gravel track opposite towards the white house. Just before you reach the house turn right at the small barn through a gate and head along the track to reach Clough House. The path skirts to the right around the buildings and enters the woods at the other side of the house. Follow the meandering path up through the dense coniferous wood and round to the right to cross over a stream after which the wood opens out and the path becomes a clear forest track all the way to the road.

Turn right along the road then almost immediately head left through a gate and drop down to join a track. Follow the track down to the left then turn right just before the gate along a grassy path passing to the right of the pond and old buildings through an area of old quarry workings.

North Dale is a hidden and unfrequented tributary valley of Rosedale with its own distinctive character, quite separate from its bigger cousin.

After the pond the path bears to the left down the hillside to reach a ladder stile, after which continue straight on to reach the road. Cross the road and walk across the field opposite, keeping close to the small ridge and wall on your left, through a wall gap then down to reach a footbridge. Cross the bridge and head straight on through a gate, then climb the small hill in front of you (do not continue along the stream) at the top of which bear to the left across the field to reach a small gate in the wall fifty yards to left of the telegraph pole. After the gate veer slightly to the left through another gate then bear to the right to reach a ladder stile in the bottom right corner of the field, marked by a signpost 'Rosedale'. Cross the stile and follow the clear path alongside Northdale Beck on your right back to Rosedale Abbey.

THE FORGE TEA SHOP

HUTTON - LE - HOLE

The highlight of this walk is undoubtedly the Norman crypt of St Mary's Church at Lastingham, which stands on the site of a Celtic monastery established by St Cedd.

TEA SHOP:
The Forge Tea Shop
Hutton-le-Hole
Tel: 01751 417444
OPEN:
Every day March –
Oct, weekends
during winter.
MAP:
OS Outdoor leisure
Map 26
DISTANCE:
7 miles (11.3 km)
ALLOW:
3 hours
PARKING:
National Park car
park at Hutton-le-
Hole.

It would be difficult to imagine a more picturesque scene with quaint stone cottages set around a rambling village green cropped short by sheep, through which flows Hutton Beck, guarded by white railings and spanned by numerous bridges. This is what attracts thousands of ice-cream-eating visitors to Hutton-le-Hole every summer, and that includes me! In the heart of the village is the Ryedale Folk Museum. This fascinating open air museum set in two and a half acres of land has thirteen historic buildings which have been carefully moved to the museum, including a heather-thatched cottage built in 1704 that was brought over from Danby and still has its original witch post by the fire to ward off evil spirits. Common land in the area is still administered by the ancient Court Leet of the Manor of Spaunton, a relic of feudal times.

From the car park head back to the road junction in the village,

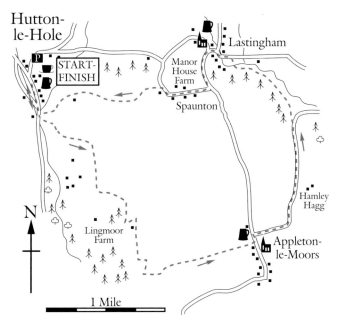

turn left along the main road and head out of the village. As the road turns to the right over Hutton Beck and leaves the village behind, take the turning to the left and follow this lane down for 50 yards where you follow the bridleway to the left marked 'Link Cropton'. Follow this track up and round to the right to reach a gate, after which continue up along the shady track as it climbs the hillside and bends round to the left then levels out. Follow the clear grassy track straight on, then round to the right and then gently downhill for a further half a mile.

As you approach Lingmoor Farm turn left off the clear track along an overgrown grassy track – do not head down to the farm. The track drops down into a secluded small valley then heads up round to the right through a small plantation to reach a gate. Head through the gate and, keeping to the perimeter of the field to the left, head across the field to a gate in the far right-hand corner of the field just to the left of the barns. Head straight on along the grassy track and follow this clear lane for one and a half miles all the way to Appleton-le-Moors.

The track passes to the left of Spaunton Quarry, a huge limestone quarry that appears to be less obtrusive than other quarries, particularly in the Yorkshire Dales, due to sympathetic landscaping. The track enters the village opposite Appleton's conspicuous church.

Appleton-le-Moors is a quiet village that presents a picture of days gone by, as this is not on the tourist map. Its single long street is lined with a mixture of old cottages, an old-fashioned country inn and a fine old hall that was once the home of Joseph Shepherd, a local man who made his fortune in the whaling business; it is now a country house hotel. The ornate Christ Church, with its 90-foot spire, was designed by renowned Victorian architect J. L. Pearson, whose other projects included Truro Cathedral in Cornwall, and was built as a memorial to Shepherd.

At Appleton turn left along the road out of the village, then take the first turning on the right towards 'Cropton, Rosedale'. Follow this road for just over a mile, bearing left at Appleton Mill Farm and left again at Hamley Hagg Farm. The road drops down passing Hagg Wood on the left, immediately after which take the path to the left through a gate. Follow the path straight on keeping close to the wood on your left, cross over a stile and carry on across the next field and through the right-hand gate ahead. The path now heads across a narrow field with Ings Beck down to the right, over a stile in the far right corner of the field and down to an old footbridge, made out of huge stone slabs over the beck, in a lovely secluded setting. A clear path leads up into the village of Lastingham.

Lastingham has been a centre of Christian worship for over 1,300 years for it was here that St Cedd, a monk from Lindisfarne, established his Celtic monastery in 654AD. Destroyed by marauding Danes in the 9th century, the monastery lay in ruins until the Norman Conquest. In 1078 Stephen, Abbot of Whitby, was granted permission to restore the monastery at Lastingham. He constructed a large crypt over the shrine of St Cedd above which he began work on the church for his abbey. However, for unknown reasons the building works were abandoned and the monks moved to St Mary's Abbey at York. The Norman crypt remains completely unaltered since the days of William the Conqueror and is unique as it has an apse, chancel, nave and aisles. The partly built abbey church was consolidated in the 13th and 14th centuries to form the parish church we see today. The altar from St Cedd's original church can still be found in the crypt as well as Anglo-Saxon crosses and Viking tombstones.

Follow the road through the village to reach the church then take the turning on the left towards 'Appleton-le-Moors' and follow this road climbing steeply uphill to reach a road junction.

On the ridge above the road stands the Victoria Cross, constructed in 1897 to commemorate Queen Victoria's Diamond Jubilee. The adjacent seat was placed there to celebrate Elizabeth II's Coronation and offers footsore walkers a superb panorama of fields, cottages with red pantiles and heather moorland in the distance.

At the junction turn right into the quiet village of Spaunton. At the far end of the village follow the road round to the right then take the track to the left over a cattle grid and head up bearing to the right towards Grange Farm. Head through the farmyard then follow the clear track to the right and round to the left to reach a group of barns. Turn left along the track just before the barns, then right along a grassy path, marked by a signpost, alongside a stone wall. Head straight on along the clear path with expansive views in all directions.

At the end of the field the path veers left then right and drops down the hillside along an overgrown path. Just after the path bends to the left take the path to the right over a stile, with views across Hutton-le-Hole's rooftops, and bear left down the hillside to pass through a gate. After the gate the path drops very steeply down the wooded hillside then runs alongside a beck and back onto the road at Hutton-le-Hole.

TREATS TEA ROOM

K I R K B Y M O O R S I D E

K irkdale's hidden Anglo-Saxon Minster and a route used by Celtic tradesmen are some of the highlights on this fascinating walk.

TEA SHOP
Treats Tea Room
West End
Kirkbymoorside
Tel: 01751 432808
OPEN:
Open every day
during summer,
closed Sun and Thurs
in winter
MAP:
OS Outdoor Leisure
Map 26
DISTANCE:
6^1/$_2$ miles (10.5 km)
ALLOW:
3 hours
PARKING:
Large pay and
display car park in
the centre of
Kirkbymoorside

There is some confusion as to the precise spelling of this town's name, as you will invariably see old signposts with 'Kirbymoorside' and more modern ones with 'Kirkbymoorside'. The name means 'settlement of the church beside the moor', which is apt indeed as there has been a church here since Saxon times and mile after mile of glorious heather moorland stretches away to the north. There was once a castle here, as street names testify; however, very little remains of this 12th century fortress. It is an unspoiled market town with many old shops, complete with old-fashioned façades, and ancient coaching inns. Just off the main street stands the elegant 17th century Market Cross in its own small square; a market is still held every Wednesday as it has done since medieval times. The town's most famous resident was George Villiers, 2nd Duke of

Buckingham, who was renowned for his high living. He died in the house known as Buckingham House on the main street and was later immortalised in the children's nursery rhyme 'Georgie Porgie'.

From the Market Place at the centre of Kirkbymoorside leave the town along West End and follow this road down to its junction with the main A170 road. Turn right along the main road, then about 300 yards after the Kirkbymoorside town sign you come to a bench. Cross the road here and head over the stile beside a gate on the opposite side of the road. Bear right down across the field, over the old railway line, and on to reach a stile in the far right corner of the field. Cross the stile and head straight across the field to reach Howkeld Mill and trout farm.

The Mill was rebuilt in the 1830s following a fire, and was still in use until the 1960s.

After the wooden footbridge head straight on through the yard, then as the track bends to the right take the footpath to the left through the wooden gate to pass in front of the old mill. Cross over the cattle grid and follow the track for a short distance then as the track bends to the right at the end of the low old brick wall head straight on across the field – no clear path – over a farm track and continue straight on to reach an old wooden fence with a line of trees.

The surrounding fields are used every July for the Ryedale Agricultural Show.

Turn right and head up alongside this dilapidated fence to reach a metal kissing gate that leads into woodland. Turn left along the lane heading towards Welburn Hall, then immediately after the ornate bridge turn right and follow the footpath through trees to a stile, after which carry straight on with Hodge Beck on your right to reach the road at Tilehouse Bridge.

This 18th century bridge was once on the main road – whilst leaning over the parapet I noticed the blue flash of a kingfisher.

Welburn Hall dates back to Elizabethan times although extensively rebuilt in 1891 and is currently used as a school for disabled children. It is a fine old building that comes as a surprise to find hidden in woodland.

Do not cross the bridge but take the path opposite over

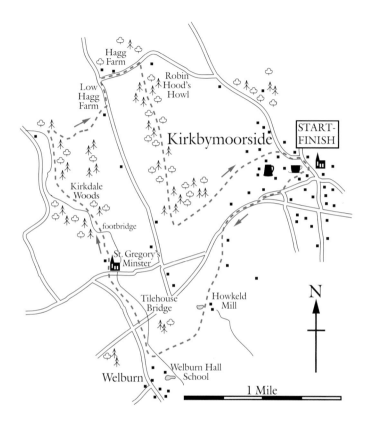

stone steps in the wall and head straight across the field
to reach the main road. Cross over the road and follow
the footpath opposite, then head across the field keeping
Hodge Beck on your right to reach a stile which leads
onto the road at St Gregory's Minster; note the railway
viaduct from the old loop from Pickering to Malton via
Helmsley.

Hidden from view amid the narrow confines of sylvan

Kirkdale, St Gregory's Minster stands as one of the ecclesiastical treasures of the North of England, famed for its Anglo-Saxon sundial, the most complete surviving Saxon inscription in the world. The inscription translates as follows: 'Orm, son of Gamel, acquired St Gregory's church when it was completely ruined and collapsed, and he had it built anew from the ground to Christ and to St Gregory, in the days of king Edward and in the days of earl Tostig. Hawarth made me: and Brand was the priest'. With so much detail still intact it is possible to date this rebuilding to between the years 1055 and 1065, although there has almost certainly been a church on this site since the 7th century.

Cross the road and follow the track opposite to reach St Gregory's Minster. Continue along the track passing to the left of the church and follow the now grassy track, keeping to the fence on your left, to cross over the beck over a wide wooden bridge after which head straight on into woodland. Follow the track up through Kirkdale Wood East, then where the track splits head along the left-hand branch. The path now meanders through woodland to eventually join a clear forest track alongside Hodge Beck.

Follow this track as it climbs steadily uphill revealing views of the thickly wooded Kirkdale. After the track has levelled out slightly, turn right back on yourself (near a telegraph pole) and follow the clear track steeply uphill. At the top of the bank turn left along a footpath over a stile in the fence then head straight across the field heading slightly to the right of Low Hagg Farm.

When you have reached the fence at the other side of the field, turn left then right through a gate and follow the track up towards the farm buildings. Cross the stile just before the farm and head straight on to join the road. Turn left along the road then take the first turning on the right along Hagg Road and follow this road passing the immaculately well kept Hagg Farm. The road drops down through a small wood, then as the road gently rises again take the path to the right over a stile that leads into woodland. A clear path follows the floor of this small valley for one mile.

This is Robin Hood's Howl, a secretive valley that is an absolute pleasure to walk through with the rich scents of the ancient woodland all around. The track along the floor of the valley was once a busy packhorse route, and may have been first used by Celtic peoples. There are numerous places within the North York Moors that claim to have associations with the famed outlaw, although evidence for this is almost non-existent.

Continue along the track until you reach a kissing gate in the fence at the end of the wood, head through the gate then immediately turn left uphill to a stile. After the stile turn right and follow the path alongside the hedge, passing Snape Wood up to your left, and follow the hedge as it bends up to the left then, as the hedge bends to the right, head diagonally across the field through a gap in the hedge halfway up the field. Follow the clear path across fields to reach a narrow path between houses on the outskirts of Kirkbymoorside that leads on to a residential road. Head straight on along the road, passing Ash Grove, then after the road has curved round to the right turn left along Sturdy Court and follow the path between the buildings to reach the main road at the top end of Kirkbymoorside.

NICE THINGS CAFÉ

H E L M S L E Y

Two hidden, thickly wooded dales take you quickly away from the hustle and bustle of everyday life.

TEA SHOP
Nice Things Café
Market Place
Helmsey
Tel: 01439 771997
OPEN:
Open every day.
MAP:
OS Outdoor Leisure
Map 26
DISTANCE:
6 miles (9.6 km)
ALLOW:
2¹/₂ hours
PARKING:
Pay and display car parks at Helmsley

It is always a pleasure to visit Helmsley. This attractive market town is the gateway to the southern North York Moors; its spacious square, complete with imposing monument to the second Lord Feversham, acts as a magnet for visitors. Interesting shops and old-fashioned inns line its streets and alleyways, which will take you eventually to the prettiest part of Helmsley alongside Borough Beck. Some of the inns date from the coaching era; in fact the half-timbered Black Swan Hotel once boasted a direct stagecoach route to London. The impressive remains of Helmsley Castle date from the 12th century. This castle was renowned throughout the country for its impregnability due to the many innovative defensive features incorporated into the design. The only test of its defensive ability came during the English Civil War when it was besieged by the forces of Parliamentarian

Sir Thomas Fairfax, surrendering only when supplies ran out. The castle was bought by Sir Charles Duncombe in 1689, whose descendants are the Earls of Feversham. Their stately home, Duncombe Park, designed by Vanbrugh, lies just outside the town.

Leave Helmsley along the lane between the Black Swan Hotel and the Crown, then at the road junction head straight on along the road opposite, marked by a signpost 'Link Carlton', and follow the path to the left of the houses up to reach the town's playing fields. After the stile at the top of the playing fields turn immediately to the right and walk alongside the fence around the perimeter of the field to reach a gate in the far corner.

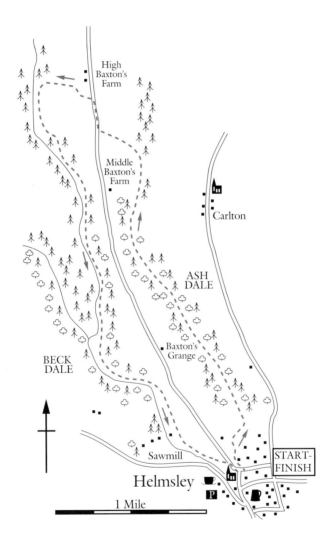

High
Baxton's
Farm

Middle
Baxton's
Farm

Carlton

ASH
DALE

BECK
DALE

Baxton's
Grange

Sawmill

START-
FINISH

Helmsley

1 Mile

Head straight on towards the next gate. However, just before this gate cross over the stile on the left and follow the path up into the woods to join a very clear forest track. Follow this track straight on heading up into Ash Dale along the valley floor for two miles.

Ash Dale is one of the many steep-sided hidden valleys that cut deep into the otherwise flat Tabular Hills that make up the southern high ground of the North York Moors. Thickly wooded with a variety of native deciduous trees, this dale is home to many species of birds, animals and insects as well as a profusion of wild flowers and plants and, unusually, does not have a stream. It is a wonderful place totally removed from the outside world. The valley gradually gets narrower and passes through an area of coniferous trees to eventually reach a junction of paths.

Turn left here, signed towards 'Baxtons', and follow the track round to the left passing through several gates to reach the road. Head right along the road towards High Baxton's Farm, then before you reach the farmhouse take the path to the left along a grassy track. Immediately before the next gate cross over the stile to your right and head up the field alongside the fence; then as this turns away to the left cross over the stile on your left and head straight on to reach a kissing gate that leads into woodland.

As you enter the wood turn left along the clear path which takes you through the wood along the top of a ridge with a steep drop down to your right. The path meanders then drops steeply down to bring you out into a small side valley. Follow the clear path down to the right to reach the bottom of the valley and a small ford across the infant Borough Beck. Do not cross the stream but head left along an indistinct path alongside the left bank of the stream to quickly reach a wide grassy path along the floor of the valley. Follow this track, crossing and recrossing the stream, for one mile until you reach a fenced off game-bird reserve.

Beck Dale is Ash Dale's sister valley but lacks the variety of trees and wildlife to be found within Ash Dale, for this is part of a large coniferous plantation. You will, however, encounter hundreds of tame pheasants and grouse bred for shooting that will follow you along the path in the hope of some food.

If the gates are open follow the track through the small enclosure, otherwise skirt to the left around it, then continue along the track into a clearing, bearing left at the junction of tracks. Follow the clear track through Beck Dale passing a sawmill after three quarters of a mile, after which the track becomes a metalled road back into Helmsley.

THE SINGING BIRD

K I L B U R N

A walk full of variety incorporating Kilburn's famous White Horse and the hidden chapel at Scotch Corner.

TEA ROOM
The Singing Bird
Teashop
Kilburn
Tel: 01347 868467
OPEN:
Every day April – Oct.
Weekends Feb – Mar.
Closed winter.
MAP:
OS Outdoor Leisure
Map 26
DISTANCE:
5 miles (8 km)
ALLOW:
2 1/2 hours
PARKING:
Parking in the small square at the front of the teashop

Kilburn is dominated by its White Horse, the only major landscape figure in the North of England, and North Yorkshire's most famous landmark visible from all quarters of the Vale of York. Unlike its counterparts in the South of England, this is not an ancient work of art, but the brainchild of Thomas Taylor, a local man who gained inspiration for his White Horse from the famous chalk horse at Uffington. He provided financial backing for the project that was undertaken by the local headmaster John Hodgson who designed and cut the figure in 1857 with the help of his pupils and local men.

In dozens of churches throughout the country mice can be found running all over the furniture, and they can all be traced back to a single source – Robert Thompson's Craftsmen of Kilburn. 'Mousey' Thompson oak furniture is now famous throughout the world for its quality and workmanship; they still use traditional tools such as the adze which gives the wood its distinctive uneven surface. Robert Thompson was a self-taught woodcarver and craftsman who received his first commission from the local priest, since when fame of his work spread. Examples of his work, particularly ecclesiastical furniture, can be found throughout the world, including York Minster, Westminster Abbey and, closer to home, St Mary's Church at Kilburn. Robert 'Mousey' Thompson died in 1955; however, the tradition continues with stacks of oak seasoning outside the workshops. The idea of the trademark 'mouse' came to him whilst he was working on a church screen as the phrase 'as poor as a church mouse' seemed very appropriate.

From the small square outside the church and teashop, turn left along the road through the village then left again just before you leave the village towards 'High Kilburn'. As the road bends sharply to the left follow the footpath to the right over a stile, marked by a signpost, and bear left across the field to reach another stile in the fence opposite. Cross the stile and follow the path steeply up to the left through the thick undergrowth, over a stile and onto an open field where the path levels out. Keep to the hedge on your left and walk across the field then head through the wooden gate/stile on the left and down to join the road through another gate. Turn right along the road and follow it round to the left, ignoring the first track to the right, then where the road turns distinctly to the left again head right along a grassy track until you come to a gate. Just before this gate there is a small metal gate on the left; head through this and follow the clear grassy track. Fine views of Kilburn's White Horse begin to open up.

This famous landmark is best seen from a distance, although its distinctive brilliant white colour is artificial as it lies on rather dull limestone; the White Horse is kept that way by plenty of chalk chippings and coats of paint.

The rough track continues straight on through two more gates after which it gradually heads to the right skirting around the base of a small hill to run alongside an overgrown hedge on the left. Just before you reach a

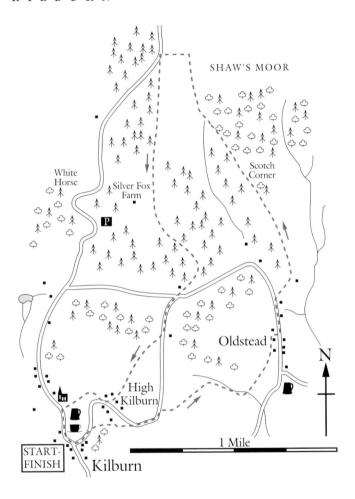

telegraph pole, turn left through a gap in the hedge, signpost 'Oldstead', and follow the path down over a footbridge, then head straight up the hillside to reach a stile in the top right-hand corner of the field. Cross over the stile and follow the hedge round to the left until you come to a gate at the end of the field. Continue straight on along the muddy farm track, through the farmyard and onto the road at Oldstead.

The monks of Byland came here in 1144 from Old Byland above Rievaulx, the noise of Rievaulx's bells forcing them to find another site. They stayed at Oldstead until 1177 when they moved a mile or so down the road to build the magnificent Byland Abbey. The monks originally called Oldstead 'Stocking', later changing the name to Oldstead, which means 'old place'.

Follow the road to the left through the dispersed village. At the fork in the road just after Sand Lane House, marked by a 'Dead End' sign, take the lane to the right and continue straight on along the rougher track – 'Unsuitable for Motors'. Follow the clear track climbing steadily upwards, with far-reaching views opening up after a while. The track levels out and crosses pastures, then heads through a gate and climbs steeply again through woodland to reach the small chapel at Scotch Corner. This tiny chapel evokes a spiritual sense of peace in such an isolated location.

The track you are walking on forms part of the old Hambleton Drovers' Road, an ancient route to the border with Scotland that has been in constant use for over 2,000 years. In 1322 King Edward II's army had returned along this road from a fruitless campaign in Scotland. They had camped out on the surrounding moors whilst their king enjoyed the hospitality of nearby Byland Abbey. Robert Bruce and an army of Scots attacked the English at night, forcing the king to flee to York and leaving the Scots to ransack

Byland Abbey. This chapel marks the spot of this bloody battle.

After the chapel continue up along the grassy track which soon levels out and becomes a clear stony track. Head straight along this track for half a mile then follow it round to the left at Shaw's Gate to reach the road. Turn left along the road and immediately take the rough track to the left, 'Unsuitable for motors'. Follow this track for one and a half miles, level at first then steeply downhill passing through woodland and the entrance to Silver Fox Farm, to reach a road. Turn right along the road then almost immediately left along the road to 'High Kilburn', and follow it down until you come to a small barn in the field on your left where you head right along a footpath to the right. Head straight uphill, bearing right then left up through an overgrown hedge, after which turn left and head alongside the hedge and plantation on your left. As the fence/wood turns away to the left, head straight on to run alongside the hedge on the opposite side of the field to reach a stile which leads on to an overgrown lane down into High Kilburn.

Kilburn actually comprises two distinct villages, High and Low Kilburn. High Kilburn's elevated position ensures wonderful views from the sprawling village green across the Vale of York, complete with old water pump, around which stand a variety of lovely old houses.

At the village green turn right along the road out of the village then as the road bends sharply down to the left take the path to the right through a white gate. Follow the path downhill keeping the fence on your right, over a farm track and straight on through the churchyard and back into Kilburn.

NATIONAL PARK VISITOR CENTRE CAFÉ

An easy stroll along level paths with exhilarating views from Sutton Bank across the Vale of York.

TEA ROOM
National Park Visitor
Centre Café
Sutton Bank
Tel: 01845 597426
OPEN:
Every day Mar – Dec;
weekends only Jan –
Feb.
MAP:
OS Outdoor Leisure
Map 26
DISTANCE:
3 miles (4.8 km)
ALLOW:
1¼ hours
PARKING:
Large pay & display
car park at Sutton
Bank

Sutton Bank provides a thrilling introduction to the North York Moors, enticing you to drive up the steep one-in-four inclines and hairpin bends, engines straining, to reach the top of the escarpment and the prospect of a vast three-dimensional map of Yorkshire beneath your feet. Alf Wight, known to millions as James Herriot, declared it to be the finest view in England – this escarpment is where his ashes are scattered. Here was also where the young William Wordsworth and his new wife Mary Hutchinson watched the sunset on their wedding night.

From the Visitor Centre walk towards the road junction at the top of Sutton Bank where you follow the footpath to the right, signposted 'Cleveland Way Sneck Yate 3 miles'. This path heads along the top of the

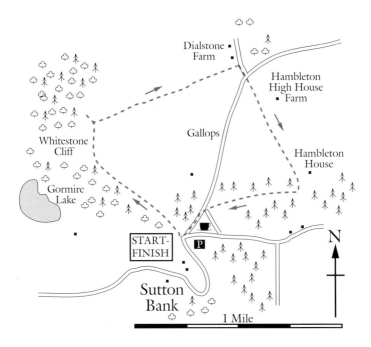

escarpment, through woodland at first then out onto the open cliff top – ignore all paths that lead down to the left.

This footpath is understandably popular due to the superb views for very little effort. On a clear day flat-topped Penhill stands guard to the broad acres of Wensleydale, Great Whernside is visible over 30 miles away and famous landmarks such as York and Fountains Abbey rise above the fertile plain. Gliders circle silently above and precipitous cliffs fall away to Gormire Lake. This glacial lake is unique as it has no streams feeding or leaving it; underground drainage regulates the flow. Many legends surround it. Local people once believed it to be bottomless, whilst another tale tells of a submerged village, including a church and spire! The Devil is also said to have lured a knight on horseback to his death over the crags at a spot still known as White Mare Crag.

After just over half a mile the escarpment (and footpath) bends distinctly to the right at which point take the path to the right back on yourself to 'Dialstone Farm'. Walk alongside the wall on your right and follow the perimeter of the field as it bends round to the left, then head straight on keeping to the edge of the field all the way to the farm.

Still a working farm, Dialstone Farm was once an inn on the ancient drovers' road known as Hambleton Street, which passed its front door. The name Dialstone refers to the weighing machine used by jockeys, as the surrounding flat

plateau, known as Hambleton Down, was once a major racecourse, eclipsing York and Newmarket. The soft turf provided perfect gallops for competitive racing which began in the early 17th century, culminating in such prestigious races as Her Majesty's Gold Cup. The isolated location meant that other racecourses with better amenities gradually won favour, although racehorses are still trained in the area.

At the farm turn right and follow the road until you reach a T-junction where you head straight on alongside the stone wall opposite heading across Cold Kirby Moor (marked by a signpost next to the road sign). Follow the wall passing the entrance to Hambleton High House Farm and on to reach the entrance to Hambleton House. Head through the white gate – walkers must stop and look before crossing the gallops – and walk on to join a gravel track then a road. Walk along the road for a short distance, signed 'Cleveland Way, Hambleton A170', then take the footpath on the right to 'Sutton Bank'. Follow the clear path through the heathland to reach a stony track where you take the footpath slightly to the right opposite. The path now meanders through an area of newly planted trees to join a clear track where you turn right to reach the road, immediately before which turn left and follow the path alongside the road on your right and Cleave Dyke on your left back to the Visitor Centre.

Not surprisingly, this elevated escarpment is rich in Bronze and Iron Age remains, particularly earthworks and dykes. Cleave Dyke was used primarily to define the boundary between tribes, indeed many of these ancient earthworks were later used by the monasteries to mark boundaries and some are still used to define parish and estate boundaries.